W9-AOP-375

"Mercy led a fascinating life. As a founding member of the GTOs, along with her relationship with Arthur Lee, she was at the epicenter of the Hollywood music scene."

—**Johnny Echols**, Love

"Mercy was absolutely the real deal, for real."

—**Blackbyrd McKnight**

"Lower Los Feliz is filled with trendy lumberjack and low fashion model wannabes, and out of nowhere there was Miss Mercy telling her stories about being in attendance at Jimi Hendrix and his *Rainbow Bridge*, watching Arthur Lee and Love in concert, a few Chambers Brothers performances and how she was the Gears' hairdresser. Mercy was the ray of sunlight cutting through gray skies and a fire opal in an ocean of gravel and rocks."

—**Keith Morris**, Black Flag, Circle Jerks, and Off!

"Mercy was my counterculture cover girl. She represented the movement of women finally staking their territory in the world of individuality, free of society's demands to conform."

—**Baron Woman**, *Rolling Stone* photographer

"Even though I met Mercy near the end of her life, I'd seen her around at different rock events over the years, always thinking, 'Who is this bold-ass woman?!' I later learned that we came from Northern California and had traveled our own musical paths, both crash-landing on the Sunset Strip in the sixties in our teens. I'm looking forward to everyone else hearing Mercy's stories and learning about her journey through her own words."

—**Brie Darling**, Fanny/Boxing Gandhis

"Back in late '78, I met Miss Mercy. To say she made me realize there was a lot more to life is an understatement. Before I knew it, I had bleached-blond hair, a large pompadour, and skateboarding was never to be the same again. She was, and always has been, important beyond most people's comprehension. Her knowledge was unmatched to most. I thank you and love you, Mercy. It's time for you to be acknowledged for the queen that you are."

—**Steve Olson**, pro skateboarder

"The women of Laurel Canyon and beyond wrote their own rules and changed them when they chose. Mercy was one of them. Her group was appropriately named because they decided they were going to be 'outrageous.' Mercy simply would not have it any other way."

—**Elliott Mintz**, celebrity publicist

PERMANENT DAMAGE
MEMOIRS OF AN OUTRAGEOUS GIRL
MERCY FONTENOT
WITH LYNDSEY PARKER

RARE BIRD

THIS IS A GENUINE RARE BIRD BOOK

Rare Bird Books
453 South Spring Street, Suite 302
Los Angeles, CA 90013
rarebirdbooks.com

Set in Warnock
Printed in the United States

10 9 8 7 6 5 4 3 2 1

Library of Congress Cataloging-in-Publication Data available upon request.

For Lucky

FOREWORD

by Lyndsey Parker

"*HOW ARE YOU STILL alive?*" That was the recurring question I'd incredulously blurt out during my nearly three years of conversations with the mythical Miss Mercy as I attempted to capture her death- and odds-defying story. "*How are you still here?*" I'd gasp as she shared tale after jaw-dropping tale of her fearless, sometimes reckless existence. But this was just a running joke between us. Because honestly, I thought Mercy Fontenot would live forever. I thought she'd outlive Keith Richards. Even toward the very end, I still thought this true soul survivor would outlive us all.

Mercy was of course best known as the most outrageous and possibly least together member of the trailblazing, Frank Zappa-produced girl group the GTOs, or Girls Together Outrageously, alongside her best friend Pamela Des Barres, author of the celebrated groupie tell-all *I'm with the Band*. When *Rolling Stone* reported the news of Mercy's July 2020 death at age seventy-one, her GTOs tenure pretty much comprised the entire obituary. But if there was ever a Zelig of rock 'n' roll, it was Mercy. When the first Acid Test went down in the Haight-Ashbury or when Jimi Hendrix made history at

Monterey Pop, she was there. When the Stones played Altamont, she was there—even though her tarot card reading for the band the night before had spelled disaster. When Al Green was a rising star in Memphis, or Wattstax took place at the Los Angeles Memorial Coliseum, or punk rock was just beginning to take over Hollywood, she was there. (She later explained to me that she knew how to gravitate toward music's "energy centers." It was one of her greatest talents. She really should have gone into A&R.)

Mercy was such a character, such a one-off—such a "threat to normalcy," as Pamela had once written—that I knew she had her own story to tell, a very different story, a story much darker than Pamela's. (When she finally agreed to work on her memoirs with me, after I'd been trying to convince her for ages, she suggested the title *I'm with the Band Too*, which I shut down immediately. But *A Threat to Normalcy* almost made the cut. I knew that Mercy's stint in the GTOs would be but one of many fascinating chapters.)

It was January 27, 2017, when it all began. Mercy rang me out of the blue to let me know she'd had a health scare and would soon be undergoing a serious operation. She wanted to see me, to say goodbye, just in case. She asked me to meet her at DJ Miles Tackett's Funky Sole Night on Broadway event at Downtown LA's Globe Theatre, where she would be serving as a dance contest judge. I have two vivid memories of that evening. One was how she cantankerously complained about the contestants' dancing skills, or lack thereof; Mercy gave absolutely zero fucks and never had a problem speaking her mind. The other memory is our ascent up to the balcony via the Globe's faded, brocade-carpeted stairwell. Mercy was ahead of me, swathed in a ridiculously molting red feather boa, trailing loose feathers in her wake. It was almost a metaphor for the colorful chaos that ensued whenever she burst into any room. Thinking this might be the last time I'd see her, I surreptitiously scooped up a fistful of feathers and tucked them into my purse. I just wanted something to remember her by.

I still have those ruby plumes, but as it turned out, there would be many memories to come. Mercy survived her surgery, just like she'd survived everything else that'd been thrown at her. But while my feather-gathering moment was the first and really only occasion when I had a sense of this larger-than-life lady's mortality, it seemed to have put Mercy in a reflective mood. So a couple weeks later, she called me again, and she called my bluff: "So, are we doing this book or what?" I guess we were, then.

I soon learned that "cantankerous" was Mercy's default—her forever mood, as the kids say. Getting her to open up and tell her stories honestly was way more challenging than I'd anticipated, especially considering how unfiltered she usually was. "*You* try remembering things that happened fifty years ago when you get to be my age," she used to bark at me when I pressed too hard. There was a guard up, a certain brittleness, which I eventually realized was the result of enduring some truly harrowing experiences that would have broken or even killed a lesser woman decades earlier. She only wept once, right in the middle of some Hollywood Boulevard fast-food joint while discussing her fraught relationship with her son, Lucky. But she quickly regained her composure, seemingly surprised by her momentary breakdown. ("Why am I crying?" she asked aloud, nervously stabbing her fries into a plate of ketchup. I knew why.)

Once when I asked her what she wanted the overall vibe or message of her autobiography to be, she shrugged and answered, "I just want it to be *fun!*" It was my job to convince Mercy that her not-so-fun stories of abuse, addiction, recovery, and redemption were just as compelling as the wacky anecdotes about her jumping out of a cake at Alice Cooper's record release party, thrift-shopping with Rod Stewart, or riding in a limo with Mick and Marianne. (Don't worry, it's all in here.)

Mercy was tough because she had to be, but there was a sweet spirit under that fearsomely steely exterior, the dozen rhinestone belts that seemed surgically attached to her twiggy hips, and the signature Theda Bara eyeliner that *Rolling Stone* once described as looking like it'd been applied with a canoe paddle. That softness came out in how she treated me and her many much-adored friends, and in her tireless evangelism of the music she worshipped—from Bobby Womack, David Porter, Esther Phillips, and Gram Parsons to her most recent obsessions: Starcrawler (who put her on the cover of their "She Gets Around" single), anything *RuPaul's Drag Race*-related, and especially Yoshiki from X Japan, who was the last rock star she really wanted to meet before she died. Her meticulously maintained Facebook wall was a virtual shrine to her favorite people, bands, movies, and TV shows. When Mercy loved something or someone, she loved with all the fierceness of the fourteen-year-old fangirl she once was. It's like she had a crush on the world. She never lost her passion. She once theorized that she had cheated death so many times because she needed to complete her mission, which was "to share some important music history with the world." That's in this book too.

Toward the end of our time working together, I asked Mercy what her favorite era of her life had been. She'd partied with Parsons in Laurel Canyon and in Hawaii with Hendrix; she'd appeared on two covers of *Rolling Stone*; she'd watched luminaries of the R&B scene in literally her own backyard while living in her father-in-law Johnny Otis's famous family home; she'd spent the seventies hanging out at the Masque and on the *Soul Train* set. But she simply cocked her head and said, "I guess my favorite era is...right now." Mercy lived every day like it was her last, until it was her last.

Mercy Fontenot *and* Lyndsey Parker

Mercy signed her book deal only eight days before she died after a long illness—the severity of which she hid from me, just like she maddeningly tried to hide so many things from me, minimizing her trauma, until I finally got her to open up. I was in denial, hoping she'd live to see *Permanent Damage* come out so she could bask in all the glory of bookstore signings and press interviews and roundtables, like the rock star she was always meant to be. I never intended this to be her last will and testament. I realize now, however, that that *was* Mercy's intention. I think once she knew her tale would be told—that she'd achieved permanence, so to speak—she felt she could finally return to whichever planet she believed was her true home.

I'm going to miss my red-feathered friend. This is her story.

PROLOGUE
This Could Be the Last Time

THE FIRST TIME I EXPERIENCED being in the news, the first time my photo was in the paper, my first taste of fame, my first connection with God...it all occurred when I was nine years old. And it was my first, and certainly not my last, brush with death.

I was vacationing with my family at the beach in sunny Sarasota, Florida, when my mother and older sister suddenly noticed I'd gone missing. "Um, I think she's dying out there," my sister announced warily, standing on the sand and pointing out to sea. I had paddled out on my boogie board way too far and found myself caught in the riptide, drifting farther and farther out, until I was just a tiny, distant dot on the horizon.

My mother was shrieking, "Save my daughter! Somebody save her!" But the lifeguards couldn't get to me. No one could. I thrashed and splashed, struggling to swim back to shore, but the waves were just too rough. My little limbs soon became fatigued; my little lungs filled with saltwater. I was only nine, and there I was, already assuming that this was it. This was the end for me.

But then, I stared up at the sky, and I prayed. Actually, it was more like I posed some sort of challenge or dare: "God, *if* you exist, please let me live." I remember thinking very strongly, "If there is a God, I will live. If there isn't, oh well, I guess I will die." But somehow, I did believe that some sort of supreme being or guardian angel would hear me.

Then, the boat came.

Over on the crest of one of those rocky waves sailed a banged-up old barge that looked just like Noah's Ark—and its captain was this silver-bearded, craggy-faced, elderly man that resembled Jesus or Moses or some sort of prophet. He intoned, "Come up and get on my boat," his booming voice sounding like it came straight out of the fucking *Ten Commandments*. I scrambled aboard, and then a helicopter descended and airlifted me back to my hysterically screeching mother on the beach.

The next morning in the local newspaper, there was an article about a little girl that had almost drowned, but a mythical mystery man—who had apparently disappeared many years earlier and hadn't been seen since—showed up out of nowhere to save this girl's life. Then the man had vanished again.

I think I saw Moses that day, I really do. And I've believed in God ever since.

I made a promise to God right then and there that I would try to lead a good and noble life. I honestly don't know how great a job I did keeping that promise. I've endured things that should have killed anybody. I've ingested every drug imaginable. I've had guns pointed at my head, needles poked in my arms. I've lived on the streets. I've gambled away much of whatever nest egg I once had. I've been raped; I've had my skull bashed in enough times to shave dozens of points off my once-high IQ; and I've battled cancer more than once. I've lived in the world of *Fear and Loathing in Las Vegas* and the world of *Requiem for a Dream*; I think I played all three real-life roles in that latter movie. And yet, maybe because of my childhood vow, I never thought I would die young and leave a good-looking corpse—that whole cliché of the 27 Club, or "I didn't think I would make it to thirty," or whatever.

Occasionally now I look back and think, "How the hell am I still alive?" I most definitely suffer from survivor's guilt, as I have been tested many times. I don't question or dwell on it too much, except when I look in the mirror and see all my wrinkles. But besides that, I thank the Lord for letting me be here this long so I can complete my mission, which is to share some important music history with the world.

My only explanation is it's simply my destiny to be here. I've always said that fate is fate. I don't even think, really, that the Moses-man saving me at sea was an act of divine intervention. I honestly believe that everything is designated, as if one's life's book is prewritten.

It took an extremely long time to write my version of that book, however, since for most of my life I was so damn high that my memories tend to blur together. And there are some traumatic episodes that I've probably suppressed in order to avoid having a total breakdown—but hey, if that coping mechanism works, it works, right? So, I can't claim to have gotten every date, name, and Wikipedia-esque detail right here. But do I really wish that I'd been sober enough to remember everything more clearly? No, not really. What would I remember? That someone dropped their drumstick? That some dude played a guitar left-handed? So fucking what? All that matters is I remember the vibe.

Mercy Fontenot *and* Lyndsey Parker

1

You're Lost Little Girl

I WAS BORN ON a date I will not print here, under a name I no longer answer to. Details like that haven't mattered in decades, anyway. When I changed my name at age fifteen, taking it from Don Covay's song "Mercy, Mercy," I was trying to escape into another person. When people call me by my real name, I don't even want to hear it, let alone print it. It reminds me of my parents.

Who knows, maybe they weren't even my real parents. My blood type is Rh negative, and this may sound insane, but there's a theory that if you're Rh negative then you're actually part alien. That would certainly make a lot of sense. It would, for instance, explain why I'm not as emotional as normal human beings. I do know for sure that I am not normal.

Regardless, I think I was born without a fear mechanism. There's a funny photo of me from when I was a little tot, maybe age four, sitting on the lap of some Easter Bunny at the mall. He's a creepy-looking, man-sized rabbit, like a mangy monster out of some *Alice in Wonderland* bad acid trip, and most kids would probably be petrified, crying and trying to wriggle away from this googly-eyed crazy creature in a cheap, matted fur suit. But in my photograph, I'm looking straight into the rabbit's dead-looking bug-eyes, laughing defiantly. There's no anxiety, no shyness. If anything, the bunnyman looks scared of *me*.

My entire childhood was spent bouncing around from city to city—Dallas, Houston, Oklahoma City, Sarasota, Denver, Seattle—so that my father could live near a racetrack, and so he could outrun his debt collectors. My father was always getting into debt and into trouble—he used to joke that his enemies wanted to put cement shoes on him, but he probably wasn't joking—so we never stayed put for very long. Dad made his living as a car salesman, or tried to, but he was hopelessly addicted to gambling and the high life. So maybe the addiction thing was in my blood—alien or otherwise. It took years for me realize how much my father and I were alike.

I wasn't very close with my dad. Nobody could be close with him. But he was a flamboyant character, larger than life, exceedingly charismatic—a strapping, handsome fellow who dressed like Johnny Cash in cowboy hats and snazzy suits, a real charmer. I did look up to him, and I kind of had a crush on him. He was a bit of a rock star himself—or I would actually describe him as a groupie. He was obsessed with TV and celebrities. Sometimes he made me sign fake autographs for him; I don't know what he did with them, if he sold them or kept them for himself to try to impress people. His chief obsession was Ann-Margret, who he claimed was his friend. I know he met her at least once because he did have a dog-eared, faded photo with her that he carried in his wallet and was one of his prized possessions. But he'd told me some tall tale about how Ann-Margret owned Marilyn Monroe's secret diaries and had tried to commit suicide, but then he found Ann and saved her. I am fairly sure he made that story up—though maybe he believed it in his pill-addled brain.

In an odd way, I was Daddy's favorite. He was a wannabe social-climber, and for me he envisioned a debutante sort of life. He wanted me to mingle with socialites at the country club. You can see how that plan worked out! He wanted to be one of the beautiful people, in with the in-crowd. He had big dreams.

Still, I don't have too many fond memories of my father. My most vivid childhood memory of him was when he brought a top *Vogue* model home—with my mother there, and while he and my mom were still married. The model, Janet, was a dazzling redhead, and I am pretty sure she was the one that got my dad hooked on amphetamines. She and my father whisked me off for a joyride that night, leaving my mom in the house alone. Later, after my father dropped me off, I ended up at a bar with my mother; she was freaked out, drinking heavily, and deeply depressed.

Another time, when I was about eight, my dad took off with me at Christmas and drove down to LA to see my favorite uncle, the film editor Warren Low. He didn't tell my mother. We almost drove off a cliff because he was so drunk. I woke up afterward and we were okay, but the authorities had to come pull us out of the wreckage. I guess that was my first brush with death, even before the near-drowning incident. I have no idea why my dad wasn't criminally charged. But my mother didn't even know we were gone.

In the early days, my mother was fashionable and extremely beautiful. She would wear tailored two-piece suits nipped in at the waist, and her shoes were really important to her. Her short-cropped hair was always neat and sprayed into a smooth, topographic shape, and her makeup was always impeccable. She was so polished and put-together—very much the opposite of the rag-tag ragdoll her freaky daughter would become. My God, she was gorgeous back then.

My mom worked long hours as a registered nurse, which was unusual; it wasn't that common back then for a wife and mother to hold down a full-time, steady job. But she *had* to, because my father was always gambling and running around with his side chicks. Somebody had to bring home the bacon, after all. And Mom's job also let her bring home a lot of pills. Sleeping pills, diet pills, tranquilizers, uppers, downers…thanks to my mother, our house looked like a pharmacy. My mom took pills all the time, but this was normal in the fifties and early sixties. Every housewife took that stuff, along with their martinis; they popped pills during their bridge games.

As for me, the first time I tried diet pills, I was about fourteen. I was heavy, so my mom took me to the doctor and got me a prescription—yep, it was as simple as that. My dad and I started to take diet pills together. My mother was a bit more controlled about it, on a regimen because she had to go to a regular job, but my father was literally necking handfuls. Soon I was as well. And the pills started to change me; I think they broadened my horizons, in good ways and bad.

I was pudgy as a kid. I had a lot of body issues growing up and was totally insecure about my weight. I started putting on weight around age eight or nine because I ate everything in the house. I ate and ate and ate. My big party trick to impress people was to eat a stick of butter whole—probably the most shocking thing a girl can do with butter this side of *Last Tango in Paris*. Maybe food was my first addiction. The first of many.

My God, I *hated* being fat. Everybody wanted to be skinny. I was just probably very shapely, now that I look back, but I considered myself obese. I tried these appetite-suppressant chocolates that were supposed to make me skinnier; I don't know what they were, but I know they didn't work. But then I did a lot of speed, and I got thin really quick. I was skinny by the age of nineteen. No more butter deep-throating for me! Nowadays I won't even put cream or full-fat milk in my coffee.

Oddly, I never drank alcohol. Booze was one thing that didn't tempt me. My father was a terrible alcoholic, and I had decided never, ever to be like him. So, I made sure that I got very sick at the age of twelve by guzzling crème de menthe until I upchucked all over the place—my own sort of amateur aversion therapy. And it worked! I rarely drank after that, maybe two or three times, and when I did I would instantly feel nauseous and have to stop. Of course, when I was twelve I had no idea that my dad was also a speed freak. Had I known, maybe I would have never gotten on speed either.

My mom was a fanatic for rock 'n' roll music, all the great rockabilly stuff: Elvis Presley, Jerry Lee Lewis, Sun Records. She was a groupie in her own way, but she didn't chase after anybody. Later when I was older, I think she was thrilled, at least at first, that I was hanging out with all these rock stars. She lived vicariously through my adventures. I even took my mom to see Janis Joplin once, and she dug it. (I, on the other hand, ran out of there screaming in terror because I was on acid and Janis's voice was too intensely witchy for my state of mind.) I once had Tiny Tim ring my mother on the phone, when he was loaded at a party after drinking all the "Beers of the World" in his refrigerator; he was drunk and rolling on the floor, but she was still excited when he called. But eventually I became so messed up that my mom became unimpressed with my rock 'n' roll lifestyle.

Growing up, we didn't have a real home. My sister, Sandra, who was five years older, hated me when we were kids. I think she was jealous that my father paid much more attention to me because I was the young and cute one (believe it or not). I remember one time when Sandra was bouncing on my pogo stick and I wanted it back, my father, who was plastered, knocked her off it, right to the ground. My sister always despised my dad for doing that—and because she thought he had drowned our pet cats. Then on my mother's deathbed, my mom told Sandra that she was the one that had killed the kitties—

my mother thought the cats had rabies and needed to be put down. My family was nuts, basically. My sister got married at fifteen just to get the heck out of there, and she ended up in and out of mental institutions for a while, though we became close in our later years.

My early childhood was not integrated. In every city we temporarily called home, the Blacks all lived on the other side of the tracks, the Mexicans only hung out with Mexicans, the Italians with other Italians, etc. Music was the one great integrating force in my life. Chuck Berry was the first rock 'n' roller I saw on *Ed Sullivan*, but the first Black artist I heard that truly affected me was Lightnin' Hopkins. I thought, "Wow, I really like that, that's cool!" It was as simple as that.

I started getting way into Black music from then on, along with soulful white artists like Dusty Springfield, Eric Burdon, and Van Morrison. I always gravitated toward Black music—although, back then, it was called "race music." Record stores used to keep it in paper bags underneath the counter. There were certain Black radio stations that were knocking down the doors and playing Black musicians, and as I bounced all over the country, I picked up all the roots music and Black channels, including XERB, a Mexican border radio station with a young DJ named Wolfman Jack. I was listening to everything from country and western all the way to the blues, and it completely expanded my mind. That's why I have a roots music obsession to this day—because I had no roots myself.

Moving around all the time was admittedly hard on me. I was a loud, attention-starved kid. I still am, I suppose. In elementary school, they wanted to put me in speech classes to soften me up, though that obviously didn't work. And my mother used to beat me with a razor strap, which is what they used back then to punish incorrigible children; that obviously didn't work either. But wherever I went, I always made friends. In the eighth grade I even ran for student body treasurer and lost by only one vote. (I did win a school Twist dance contest that same year, which, of course, was more important to me.) But eventually, when I was about fourteen, my family settled in the Northern Californian suburb of San Mateo in the Hillsdale Garden Apartments due to their convenient proximity to the Bay Meadows Racetrack. It was there that I met two very important friends, Monte Moore and Ricky Prescott, who truly sent me on my path. Or maybe we were already going down the same path, and it was our destiny to travel it together.

There were four of us, a girl named Linda being the other one, and Linda had a cousin that was supposedly working for all the British Invasion bands. And supposedly those bands were writing us letters. Every week, we'd receive a big packet full of mail from the Rolling Stones, the Beatles, and the Animals, and we would excitedly answer back on our girly, scented, pink stationery. The letters came postmarked from England and seemed legitimate, though to this day I don't know who was really writing them. Maybe it was all a scam. But through that, Ricky, Monte, and I forged a connection. And I quickly morphed into Ricki Lake's character in *Hairspray*, obsessed with all things music, with Mom's uppers racing through my teenage bloodstream and only intensifying the radio waves that called to me through Wolfman Jack, Tom Donahue, XERB, and KSOL.

In 1965, the girls and I went to this hotel where we'd heard the Beatles were staying. We got a room, checked in, and I slept in the bathtub. We never met the Beatles that day, and we didn't even really try; we just wanted to be close to them. That same year, we went to Sacramento's Memorial Auditorium to go see the Stones, who were playing with Patti LaBelle and the Bluebelles. Keith Richards got electrocuted onstage; the curtain fell down and the whole concert came to a crashing halt. We hopped in the car and followed the Stones, to see if Keith was all right. We didn't realize he wasn't in the car—the Stones had switched cars to fool crazy fans like us, and Keith had been taken to the hospital on his own. Still, we trailed the band all the way back to their little bungalow hotel in Sacramento, and this time we got much closer to our idols.

Early on, I was atomically attracted to the fame frequency. My earliest rock 'n' roll memory is meeting the Ink Spots as age seven and asking them for their autograph. I was at a bowling alley with my dad and spotted them. After that, I dreamed of meeting the Beau Brummels, and I willed it into reality: I was in a restaurant with my mother and there they were, the Beau Brummels, eating dinner next to us. I dreamed up everyone I wanted to meet—and I had long dreamed of meeting Brian Jones. So that night after the Stones' ill-fated show in Sacramento, we ended up in Brian's hotel room. He had his door open, so we simply walked right in, and he let us; I guess we seemed harmless enough to him. He was a sweetheart. I just sat there in silent awe and watched him rummaging through his suitcase and all his exquisite rock 'n' roll clothes. I loved Brian with all my heart, but I didn't know anything about sex or anything. I was too young to care about wanting to sleep with him; I was content just to look at him and be in his presence. I would become friends with Mick Jagger and Keith Richards in a few years' time, but tragically Brian is someone I never really got to know. However, I was actually wearing Brian Jones's coat, lent to me by my boyfriend Jobriath, when I found out Brian had died in 1969. I was devastated by the news. I had been writing my diaries to Brian for years.

MONTE MOORE WAS A real trip. She was *fab-u-lous*. She was a beatnik, a rich chick, and both of her parents, who were never around, were morphine addicts. I used to call her the "morphine orphan." She had Keane-painting eyes and dressed like a little elf, with a cape and pointy shoes and waist-length, stick-straight hair perfectly parted down the middle. She smoked pot all day in her basement and listened to Gil Evans and Django Reinhardt and all the jazz cats. I had a massive, dopey crush on her. Monte was the one that took me to North Beach, which was a whole other scene before the hippies took over. The beatniks were anti-*everything*, and I loved that. They listened to folk singers, played chess, wrote poetry, and were brooding and mysterious and sophisticated and hip. I loved North Beach, with soul music and jazz and folk and Chicago blues blasting out of all the record shops, along with Bob Dylan moaning his words of wisdom. Monte introduced me to that entire magical world, whisking me off to the Blue Unicorn—the cool folk hangout in San Francisco.

The Blue Unicorn is where I grabbed the first boy I went to bed with when I was fifteen, Frank. At least I think his name was Frank. He could have been anybody, really. He could have been Jack Kerouac, for all I know. He was a hunky, motorcycle-driving beatnik, light-haired and more manly than I usually went for, probably about twenty-five years old. I can't claim that our one-night stand was romantic or earth-shattering or anything like that. We just clambered up to the Blue Unicorn's cavernous attic piled with beds, mattresses laid out end-to-end on the floor, and had sex. It was nothing to me; I merely wanted to experience it and get it over with. I remember thinking, "Wow, this hurts. Is that all there is?" But then I figured, "Well, at least I did it." Frank was a nice guy, though—it wasn't like he knocked me down on a bed or made me do anything I didn't want to do—and afterward, he even gave me a ride home on his motorbike. Sex to me was boring. It wasn't until I was in my late twenties that I finally found out it could be incredible.

Monte took me to the Longshoreman's Union Hall's famous first Acid Test Festival, organized by counterculture author Ken Kesey in January 1966 to celebrate all the glories of this new-fangled drug called LSD. I don't recall very much about it. I remember Allen Ginsberg babbling zany stuff and ringing his bells and cymbals with his fingers, *ding, ding, ding*, while I was dancing. All I remember is that and the light show. I think someone dropped something in my drink because at all these far-out hangouts, the beatniks and hippies were spiking everything. I hadn't tried LSD myself yet, but a couple weeks later, Monte would change all that.

One night Monte and I were taking a car ride back from North Beach, and she gave me a tablet. She said, "Take this," and I did because I idolized her and would have done anything she told me to do. A few minutes later, she yelled, "You have lemons in your mouth!" She put that notion in my head, and I just couldn't shake it. She was right—I could feel the pulp, taste the sour sting of the juice. My vision then started to pixelate and blur into tracers. Then Monte unceremoniously dropped me off at my house, and I was left alone in my bedroom.

I collapsed on my frilly twin bed, trembling, staring at my many Gypsy bracelets metamorphosing into snakes and slithering up my chubby arms. The walls started breathing; my parents' whispers down the hallway were echoing, making my bedroom walls vibrate and undulate with their every word. I glanced out my window and I saw a carnival downstairs on the driveway, complete with a Ferris wheel, clowns on stilts, sideshow acts, fireworks, and a raging funhouse. Then I dove inside my transistor radio, which I suppose in retrospect was a metaphor for my life. I went inside my little portable radio and wandered around. There were bands inside; every time a song would play, that band would be in the radio, standing right in front of me. *That* part was fabulous; the rest was terrifying. I thought I was losing my damn mind. I was scared senseless because nobody knew much about LSD yet, so I had absolutely no idea what was happening to me.

Mercy Fontenot *and* Lyndsey Parker

The next day, still spooked, I went outside to walk it off, and the sidewalks were shifting beneath my feet. I went over to my girlfriend Beverly's house and I told her, "*Never* take LSD!" Of course, I would soon go on to ignore my own advice and drop acid all the time. As petrified as I'd been by this trip, I was ultimately lured in by the unknown. Just like my body after the attic encounter with Frank the beatnik, my mind was no longer a virgin. Nothing would ever be the same. Besides, I'd soon be living in Haight-Ashbury...and in the Haight, people did acid whether they wanted to or not. That's just how it was. LSD was anywhere and everywhere and unavoidable.

I left my parents' house at age fifteen, just like my sister Sandra before me. My mother was heartbroken. She was trying so, so hard to understand me, but I was long gone in my mind. She'd already lost her oldest daughter, and she really didn't have a husband, and now here I was going off the deep end. But I couldn't stay, especially after I came home late one night and my father tried to strangle me, claiming I was killing my mother with the reckless life I was leading. He sure was one to talk.

Unlike my sister, however, who'd escaped into a child-bride marriage, I escaped to San Francisco. Ricky Prescott was a grade ahead of me, and when she moved there, I happily followed and shacked up with her. Ricky was another one of my major girl crushes: a vision in gossamer vintage dresses, her flowing hair festooned with dozens of fresh flowers. Haight-Ashbury was this mecca of Victorian houses that could be rented for practically nothing, like fifteen rooms for fifty dollars a month, and our neighbors there were incredible—I mean, we'd be in a house with Janis Joplin literally rehearsing downstairs.

When I arrived in Haight-Ashbury, I felt like I finally had a home, there with my fellow outcasts, the Fellini people, in the freak zone. We all looked like we'd stepped out of a dream. And it *was* a dream—until it became a nightmare.

2

Luv R' Ħaight

EVERYONE THINKS THE HAIGHT-ASHBURY was so glorious and glamorous, but it wasn't all peace, love, and understanding—the mob was moving in and knocking off my friends, sawing off my friends' arms because they were independent drug salesmen, stuffing people into car trunks. I had guns pulled on me all the time. It was hardly the Summer of Love. The "Summer of Love" was just a tourist attraction to me, something *Time* magazine made up. The flipside, the dark side, was always going on.

There were some amazing times, of course. The love-ins were fantastic fun, except I had to see the Grateful Dead all the time, and I was never a Deadhead. But there was Blue Cheer, who were just tremendous, and at places like the Avalon and the Fillmore you could actually see Blue Cheer on the same bill with someone like Muddy Waters or Jimi Hendrix. It was a big mixture of everything and everyone I loved. However, one of the worst drug experiences I ever had was at the Avalon Ballroom.

Roky Erickson and the 13th Floor Elevators were playing the Avalon that night, and I decided to pay forward what Monte Moore had done for me and help this naive young hippie girl embark on her first acid trip. I took half of the tab myself, then gave the girl the other half. All of a sudden, my whole world started turning acid-green, the color of puke. I hobbled up a long, creepy staircase in a lysergic panic, and Chet Helms, who managed Janis Joplin and worked at the Avalon, took one look at me and could tell what was up. He said, "Look, you've been poisoned. The acid out today is cut with strychnine. People are dying. But I think you'll be okay. Come with me *right now*. Come up to this room." Chet dragged me up the rest of the steep stairs and stuck me up there where they put all the freak-out cases. I'd never known this comedown room existed before. Chet commanded, "Just deal with it," and left me alone to chill.

I could see the stage through a tiny dirty window, and I was watching the 13th Floor Elevators play "It's All Over Now, Baby Blue" by Bob Dylan. I felt like I was dying all by myself up there. It sounded like a death song, with lyrics like "the carpet, too, is moving under you" and "you must leave now, take what you need, you think will last." I was sprawled out on the cramped room's tattered, stained carpet as the slanted ceiling closed in on me, helplessly thinking, "Okay, this is it. This is the end. It's all over now, baby blue." I don't recall making a bargain with God that day. I just accepted it this time.

But eventually the effects of the bad acid started to wear off, so I figured I better find this girl that I took on her first trip and see if she was all right. I stumbled downstairs and clutched at her and exclaimed, "How are you handling this? Are you okay?" She raved, "God, that was really fun! I loved it! I want more!" Evidently, I must have got the half with all the strychnine in it, or this chick was just crazy.

Death always seemed right around the corner in San Francisco. Sometimes it was literally next door. One time in the Victorian I shared with Ricky, I could hear Charles Manson in the adjacent room, talking to a Black guy about the "blood wars" that would soon erupt due to all the racial unrest in the world. I was sky-high on really good LSD, and I kept hearing Manson's lecture seeping through the wall about how there was going to be a race war, race riots, blood flooding the streets. The words went in one ear and out the other, but then finally they got drilled into my strained brain. Charlie sounded very matter-of-fact about this whole deal, like he was really just trying to warn this dude about what was inevitably going to happen. He didn't sound threatening or anything, more like he was just stating facts. To be honest, he wasn't entirely wrong.

This was a couple years before the Manson murders. Later a friend of mine went down to Spahn Ranch and came back and told me that Charlie Manson knew I was a vegetarian at the time. "He knows everything you do," my friend warned me. I shrugged. It didn't make any sense to me. "Well, that's nice," I said. Then I probably ate a salad.

Another time I was visiting a friend's place while he was copping drugs, and I heard this tiny peep of voice in my head that said, *"Don't do it. Don't do the deal."* I've heard that voice many other times in my life, and it has saved me or saved someone else. I told my friend, "Listen, don't go through with this drug deal." But he ignored me. Then I heard my inner voice say, "You shouldn't really do this...*but it's going to be okay.*"

We had just tried some speed. There came a knock at the door and the DEA busted in—and I had the box with *all* the drugs. We were on the second floor and luckily I threw the box right out the window, just in time. But the police still came *straight* for me, with guns aimed at my skull: "Don't move or we'll blow your fucking head off!" One of the detectives was different, however—kinder. I said to him, "Look, officer, sir, I'm trying to get off drugs. I really don't want to do this anymore." I was full of shit, of course. But this cop took pity on me. He said, "I have a daughter your age. We're just going to let you go."

He escorted me out the door while my friend got arrested. It was a trip, the way that all happened. Some would say the voice in my head had steered me wrong that night, but it actually *was* all okay in the end—after all, I didn't get my head blown off. I think I expected something was going to happen; I just walked into it on purpose because I knew it would be all right.

Probably my favorite San Francisco memory was the Monterey Pop Festival. Somebody scored me a spare VIP pass, so I went backstage and drank some of the punch. Tiny Tim was back there, Brian Jones was back there, the Who were back there, along with their gorgeous girlfriends. I talked to Brian for a minute, asked him what sign he was—probably the stupidest thing I could have ever said to him—and then suddenly I was as high as ten kites. I think Owsley from the Grateful Dead's entourage put STP in the punch; that was a three-day government high. This stuff was probably why Hendrix got so wild onstage, and probably why by the time the Who got on, they'd totally lost their minds.

At some point that day, I remember hearing this weird sound. I was way out in the field somewhere, and I said, "What is that? It's like an extraterrestrial thing." I came back and it was Jimi onstage. Two days later, still wasted out of my gourd, I'd see Buddy Miles and Jimi Hendrix, still jamming in a hotel room. This was Jimi before I really knew Jimi. Brian Jones had brought him to the hotel. I looked up these stairs and I thought, "There's Brian, and I guess that's Mick Jagger in blackface"—which turned out to actually be Jimi, not Mick. *That* is how high I was.

I was with Janis Joplin's drug dealer the night she died, though by that time I had moved down to Los Angeles. Her dealer was named Jean de Breteuil and he was in the phone book and everything. I wasn't really that into heroin, though once in a while I'd do it because I would take anything offered to me, any drug—it didn't matter what it was. I was living on La Brea Avenue in Hollywood, and Jean came to visit me, bringing me the same heroin he had just given Janis. You know that saying, "go placidly amid the noise and haste," from the Max Ehrmann poem? Janis had just recited that to Jean. He said, "I wonder why she told me this." Then he said, "I have this dope and I want to shoot you up with it, and I'm going to watch you." He wanted to test the smack on me, basically use me as his guinea pig. Naturally, I was up for the task. But as soon as he shot me up, I knew something had gone very wrong.

I shouted, "I'm going down *way* too fast. I'm just going *down*. Help!" So Jean gave me a shot of cocaine to snap me out of it.

Neither of us knew at the time that Janis would overdose from this same batch of heroin. Jean left the smack with me, but it was so strong, I couldn't handle it, so I gave it to my junkie pal Gram Parsons. I didn't sell it to Gram or anything; I just didn't want it in my possession. But then the guy with Gram OD'd, so we had to call our friend Chuck Wein to come bring that dude back to life. Later that night, Janis died around two o'clock in the morning. When I heard the news on the radio, I said, "Oh, yikes. Whoops." It was very sad. Janis was only two blocks away from me. She actually passed away in a hotel that my band GTOs lived in before, the Landmark. But I'll get into my GTOs, Gram, and Chuck stories later.

Jean was seriously freaked out. I know he did not mean for that to happen to Janis. I don't know how it happened, exactly. I've been told that Janis had an amulet around her neck that usually stored cocaine in it in case she had too much heroin, and that one of her girlfriends had changed it to more heroin—so when Janis went to do the coke shot, she overdosed on smack instead. That's one story. I cannot definitively say. I've always suspected it was a setup and Jean was caught in the middle, but I can't confirm that either.

Mercy Fontenot *and* Lyndsey Parker

After Janis died, you would've thought I'd have some sort of holy-shit epiphany, a there-but-for-the-grace-of-God-go-I sort of thing. But it didn't scare me in the least. Everybody could've dropped dead around me—and a lot of people did eventually, like Jimi and Gram—and it wouldn't faze me. All I thought about was getting high, high, higher. When you're addicted to drugs, that is how your brain functions, or malfunctions. Yes, I thought maybe it was a possibility I could end up like Janis, but the prospect didn't bother me since I believed in that whole prewritten-fate thing.

Meth was actually my drug of choice in my Haight-Ashbury days, more than heroin or LSD or anything else. First of all, it made me lose weight, so that was nice. And it made everything beautiful. The first time I ever did it, I felt like I had gone to heaven. It was the greatest rush in the whole wide world. It felt exactly like I'd thought sex was *supposed* to feel: this warm, whole-body-orgasm sensation that traveled from my feet all the way up to my head and then back down to my feet again. That *feeling* was the addiction, not the drug itself. I had a good run with speed for about three years, but then it went into reversal and every time I tried to get high, it no longer did what it had done for me before. And the comedowns were pure agony after being high for a few days, which, of course, is why I kept trying to chase that original high.

Speed became my lifestyle and even defined my fashion sense. My "Miss Mercy" persona, if you want to call it that, was truthfully the product of a bunch of speed. I would get high and keep piling clothes on top of clothes and eyeliner on top of eyeliner until I looked like Theda Bara. I would go for days without sleeping or washing my eyeliner off, and it would become blacker and blacker. I became known for this sooty look—when *Rolling Stone* wrote about all the groupies backstage at Altamont, they captioned my photo with "Most dazzling: Miss Mercy behind her raccoon-ring eye makeup."

Once I had eye surgery and couldn't wear makeup for ten days. Oh, my God, that was the worst. The entire time I was recovering, I felt like screaming, "Where are my eyes?"

I wore heaps of scarves and belts and bracelets—the same bracelets that had turned into snakes when I did acid the first time—everywhere I went, so I'd be able to walk into any bathroom and tie off my arm any time I wanted to shoot up. There was an amusing line that my friend Marlowe B. West wrote in his memoir, *Go West, Young Man*. He said when he first met me, I was sitting on a bed, and when I got up, all the bedding went with me. He thought it was blankets and sheets, but it actually was the layers of clothing that I was trailing. I had kept all my clothes on because I couldn't run around with a bag and I was never home or in one place for very long. So I was basically a suitcase on legs, a walking wardrobe.

A lot of the San Francisco girls dressed what you would call "steampunk" today. There were many girls like me who dressed, for all intents and purposes, in drag. Me, the Cockettes and Fayette Hauser, Ricky Prescott—all of us freaks were Gypsied-out in our tattered ballgowns and velvets and silks. Janis Joplin actually was quite plain before she got around us. The media would show Haight-Ashbury hippies with greasy hair and stupid bellbottom pants, but that's not what was really happening.

I remember once I went with my mother to the mall. People would stare, and somebody looked at me and said to her, "Is this Halloween?"

My mother became enraged and barked, "Don't you dare talk to my daughter like that!" She got very defensive. It was actually quite cool of her. She still was a good mother to me, or as good as she could be, while all this was going on.

Once I was shooting speed in Haight-Ashbury and somebody gave me five Stelazine, which is a muscle relaxer, because I really needed some rest; I'd gone three days without a wink of sleep. I had no idea what Stelazine did, but I took all five of them, of course. I woke up the next day and went to Golden Gate Park, and suddenly my jaw felt like a typewriter—it was shifting back and forth sideways, like when you hit a typewriter at the end of a sentence, and every time my jaw would move to the right, I would scream out in pain. And then I went into seizures. I was with a friend known as Peter Pan, and I told him, "You need to call an ambulance. *Now.*"

Somehow I made it to the emergency room, and the doctor there warned me, "If you scream one more time, we're going to have you arrested." And he called my mother to come collect me.

My mother marched in, and being a registered nurse, she went right up to the doc and said, "If you ever speak to a patient like that again, I swear I will do something about it."

My mom carted me home and stuck me in a bathtub—and that was when she found a bunch of holes in my arm. My poor mother had to see me with needle marks all over, looking like a life-size voodoo doll. She wasn't a particularly religious Catholic, but in that moment she took out her rosary and began to pray. She didn't know what else to do other than sob.

My seizures continued, so my mother drove me to the San Mateo Hospital, where she was the head nurse, and I was checked into the psychiatric department and given some Thorazine. They gave me so much Thorazine that I felt like I had weights on my feet and was underwater, drowning; it took me right back to that Florida beach at age nine. I could see from above what was happening to me; I was watching my body from above me, and I don't know if I was out of my body, meaning that I was almost dead, but the Thorazine did eventually stop the seizures. And I lived.

And then...I went right back to the Haight. It was there that I met my first boyfriend and one of the most important people in my life, Bernardo Saldana.

Bernardo wasn't a musician, but he was one of the biggest rock stars I ever knew. He wasn't an actor or model, or anything like that, either; he never did anything but look beautiful, but that was enough. He was the most popular and fine-looking boy in Haight-Ashbury. He was more of a boy-girl, really. He a walking god, a walking goddess, a stunning and strong-featured Latin prince/princess who dressed in exotic garments—jeweled bracelets and embroidered boleros and vintage velvets. He looked like Cleopatra, like a Charles Dickens character, like an exquisite creature from a fairy tale. He'd strut into any room and people would flock to his side, just to be near him. Even straight guys went for him. I would have followed him anywhere and everywhere. Eventually, I followed him down to LA.

I don't even recall how Bernardo and I first met. But somehow in our Haight haze we did, and before I knew it he was my old man and I was his old lady. He was the first love of my life. I was seventeen, he was nineteen. We didn't actually go to bed together, other than in the literal sense. But he was my soulmate and my rock 'n' roll-mate because sometimes I felt like a man, and I *know* he felt like a woman. Bernardo had other girlfriends, and boyfriends too—he was known as a "BTO," one of the Boys Together Outrageously—but I was his number one, and together we were breaking all the barriers.

Bernardo and I were always gussied up and always out on the town. We were *the* it-couple of Haight-Ashbury. I suppose if the term "influencer" had existed back then, that was what we were. We were style stars. Shopgirls in boutiques used to give us free clothes, which I would, of course, layer on top of the clothes I already had on. Bernardo and I were even on the sixth cover of *Rolling Stone*, in a prize-winning photo from the famous Gathering of the Tribes, of the "Human Be-In"—an iconic image that bound us together forever.

It was that day that Baron Wolman, the legendary chief photographer for *Rolling Stone*, spotted us in Golden Gate Park. "Can you just pose for us? I like your looks," he said simply, and he snapped that historic photo. I didn't think much of it at the time. A few weeks later I was high on acid at the Fillmore, and I saw the issue there and went, "Oh, my God, Bernardo. We're in *Rolling Stone!*" I could not believe it. There I was on the cover in my white poet blouse, perfectly worn-in 501 Levi's, and antique fur coat, staring and glaring right at Baron's lens with my kohl-caked eyes. Exactly a year later, on my birthday, I was in *Rolling Stone* again—issue No. 27, the "Groupie" issue—this time taking up the entire back cover.

It was always romantic with Bernardo, even if we didn't have a physical connection until much later. But the platonic thing was fine with me. Even though I'd already had sex with that beatnik back at the Blue Unicorn, I didn't care about sex that much. Falling in love was more important. And I was deep, deep in love with Bernardo. Eventually, we did consummate our relationship in the seventies. I don't even know how, or why, it happened. I was in San Francisco visiting him, and suddenly he wanted to do it, so I said okay. I wasn't really in love with him anymore, so it wasn't very amazing and it was all kinds of awkward and strained. I'd say it didn't live up to my expectations, but I didn't really have any expectations. There was no need for that to ever happen again. But if that had happened in 1967, I probably would have lost my mind.

Not all my adventures with Bernardo were so thrilling. I had a girlfriend, Bonnie, who'd just got out of jail, and one night she came out with me and Bernardo to the Avalon and I introduced her to a Hells Angel named Buck. At the end of the night, Bonnie, Bernardo, and I wound up in Oakland at the Angels' house there. Bernardo and I were in one room, just hanging out, and then some Angels busted through the door and proclaimed, "We're going to rape you, and we're going to kill him." We were terrified, or more just in a state of shock. But before anything could happen, this mountain of a man named Teeny, who was like six foot eight and very respected among the Hells Angels, swooped in and said, "Don't touch 'em. You'll do no such thing." It was like that scene in the movie *The Wanderers*. Teeny had no reason to stop our would-be rapists/murderers from having their way with us other than he was a good person. Teeny drove me and Bernardo back to where we were staying, and that was that. Crisis was averted. Bonnie stayed behind, for some reason—I think she wanted to introduce speed to the Angels. Hopefully she made it out of there all right; I never saw her again.

It was around this time that I met one of my other great loves, my girlfriend Sapphire. Like Bernardo, she was an exotic and erotic beauty, an Armenian girl with cascading black hair and feline eyes who was always in and out of foster homes. She was the first girl I ever truly loved. Oh, I had *such* a crush. I think she may have had a crush on me too, but I can't say for sure. I used to talk to Sapphire about marrying her, but I only made out with her once. It was another one of those platonic situations where when you're near somebody, that's all you really need, and if you actually have sex, it can wreck everything and actually bring down the fascination with the person. But if I'd had the chance to cross that line, I totally would have.

Sapphire and I were always together. Even when I got thrown into juvenile hall, which was often, the authorities made sure they gave us the same room. One time, Sapphire and I were spending the night at Hillcrest Juvenile Hall—which, true to its name, was on a very high hill—when all of a sudden our room was illuminated with a blinding light that stirred us from our slumber. I looked through the window, down at the playground outside, and there was a hovering flying saucer, like something out of an Ed Wood movie. And then suddenly we were within the silver walls of the steel ship, staring at each other, and the aliens were talking in colors, telling us, "Walls cannot hold your soul." I said to Sapphire, "Do you *see* this? Do you see what I am seeing?" And she said yes. And then we teleported out of there, like *Star Trek* holograms that had been beamed up.

And, no, we were *not* on drugs. There were no drugs in juvenile hall.

Nobody besides me and Sapphire had this close encounter of the third eye, so I don't know if we were the only humans allowed to see it. But later, after I got out of juvie, people would come up to me and say, "Hey, it was really fun running into you here last week"—and I *hadn't* been wherever they thought they'd seen me. So I think I learned how to transcendentally time travel that night in juvie. People would tell me all the time, "I swear I saw you." One woman would bring me posters from the Avalon and the Fillmore, and I could actually look at them and *go* there in my mind. So, maybe I really am part alien. And maybe some distant green relatives were trying to visit me that fateful evening.

When I wasn't in and out of juvie, by age seventeen I was mainly living with Ricky Prescott, and one night a probation officer stopped by my family's home in San Mateo and told my parents they needed to check up on me. My mother called me and said, "You need to get back here. Don't worry, the cops are just here to talk to you. They're not going to do anything." Of course that was a big fat fucking lie. The minute I walked into my parents' house, the authorities slapped handcuffs on me and placed me under arrest for breaking some sort of probation. That's when I hollered, "I'm not going back to juvenile hall! You can just take me to the mental hospital! I'm crazy!" I guess it wasn't too hard for the officers to believe I legitimately might be insane in the membrane, so off I went.

I actually preferred the mental hospital over juvenile hall because I had much more freedom there; in juvie, you had no rights, but in the mental ward, friends could come visit you, and you could have a lot of fun. So I decided that was where I wanted to stay, and I concocted my master plan. While high on Thorazine, I took a shard of glass and scraped straight across my wrist with it. It was not a real suicide attempt. And I wasn't scared to do it. I was so high that I was numb, watching with fascination as my own blood spurted up to the ceiling. It didn't even hurt. I wasn't frightened of death to begin with, but I also knew the hospital staff would find me in a second anyway and make sure I didn't die.

Unfortunately, the doctors called my bluff. "How dumb do you think we are?" they said as they rolled their disapproving eyes. And then they got really furious at me because some other patient saw what I did and copied me. So my stay in the mental ward only lasted a few days. The doctors dispatched me right back to juvenile hall, where I got sentenced to two years. I still have the wrist scar, though.

I was in juvie for about three months this time around. I was told I could leave on my own recognizance if I promised to stay home and go to school, but of course that did not last. I actually got myself arrested in juvenile hall. Basically, I said I didn't want to live with my parents anymore, so I went to the courthouse and was deemed so "incorrigible" that they made me a ward of the court. But that genius plan backfired too. Once I was a ward of the court, I was informed that I would be shipped to the Youth Authority, which was actually much, much worse than juvenile hall. YA was a nightmare, a real lock-up, a real prison, and it would have sent me down a very bad path. That's where a hardened criminal career really begins.

I was treated quite well in juvie, all things considered. My probation officer absolutely adored me and would bring me care packages and treats, plus I usually had Sapphire with me. Monte Moore ended up there too; I recall how happy I was when my probation officer came in and said, "I have good news; your friend Monte has come to stay!" One day that guardian-angel probation officer came to me with even better news. She'd taken pity on me, so she told me, right before I was supposed to get sent to the Youth

Authority: "Look, we're going to let you be the first person to test our new program. We'll let you go home for a day to get yourself together. I'm going to make sure that you get a day off before you go, so you can go shopping and say your goodbyes and whatever." It was a real sweet deal, and it was truly kind of her to stick her neck out for me like that.

I was supposed to go home to San Mateo to see my family. So what did I do? I bought a plane ticket to Orange Country for ten dollars and hopped on a midnight flight—headed to Laguna Beach, about fifty miles south of Los Angeles, where Bernardo was staying. I just ghosted. And I stayed away until after I turned eighteen. I was like one of the Shangri-Las: I could never go home anymore. I had no home. Bernardo would be my new home.

My probation officer was a marvelous person. I probably screwed everything up for her and everybody else. I'm sorry.

3

L. A. Woman

I DIDN'T LIKE Los Angeles, or at least the *idea* of Los Angeles, at all at first. I never expected to live there. I was a proud NorCal gal, and San Francisco had a rivalry going on with LA, and I was dumb enough to buy into that cliché of "Hollyweird." I remember one night with Jimi Hendrix at the Fillmore, I had given him a beautiful, hand-painted ivory bracelet, little square tiles strung together on elastic with Japanese calligraphy and illustrations, which I later saw him wearing all the time in press photos. That same evening, he asked me to introduce him to a pretty girl at the club; he wanted me to be his wingwoman, to use a modern term. "Please go get her for me," he pleaded. I went over to try to talk to her, but then I found out she was from LA, so I marched back and started yelling at Jimi: "Why in the world would you go out with some Hollywood dame? They are so fake and plastic! You don't want a chick from Los Angeles. You go and get yourself a nice girl from San Francisco!"

But then, one night the Doors were playing the Fillmore in San Francisco, and I experienced an encounter that made me rethink the whole anti-Los Angeles thing. Ricky Prescott and I were still living with a bunch of other girls in our beautiful Victorian house, and the Doors' drummer, John Densmore, was dating one of our roommates. Jim Morrison's girlfriend Pamela Courson and John came over, and Pamela was trying to crawl into a little mouse-hole in our wall because she was on acid and thought she was Alice in Wonderland. She kept crying out, "I need to get in here! I need to go in there!" No one tried to stop her. Maybe we all wanted to watch and see if she'd be able to do it. We were probably all on acid too, come to think of it.

Eventually we calmed Pamela down, and we proceeded to tag along with her to the Doors' Fillmore rehearsal. The place was empty except for Jim Morrison, sitting in the audience area alone. He looked like a romantic, a pirate, a dandy, a poet, with his shoulder-grazing Tarzan hair and square jaw and cut-glass cheekbones and white ruffled blouse and black leather trousers with the turquoise studs running up the sides. I was in awe. I marveled to myself, "Oh, my God, if people from Hollywood look like *that*, then I'm going to have to change my mind about going there!" And I did adjust my attitude from that point on. And then a couple years later in LA, I saw Jim on Sunset Boulevard with his scruffy beard and bloated face, looking like a lumberjack and weighing about 200 pounds, and I thought, "Damn, what the fuck happened to him?"

Before I made it to LA proper, after my juvie escape, I first landed in Laguna Beach because Bernardo was there. It was easy to track him down because Bernardo was popular and known wherever he went. Laguna was postcard-pretty, but it had the wildest, most out-of-control drug scene, thanks to this LSD cult called the Brotherhood of Eternal Love. The place was just teeming with drugs. It was in Laguna that I had my first experience shooting up speed with an ether base, so I got addicted to that really fast. Anyway, I had no money, but I had Bernardo, so I was set; we scammed our way through, thanks to his charm and the kindness of Bernardo-smitten strangers.

Everybody wanted to take care of Bernardo, to cater to him. And then I followed Bernardo to Hollywood. Much to my surprise, I loved it. It was fabulous. The only thing that made LA different from San Francisco was the skirts were shorter.

When we arrived in Hollywood, we were greeted by these elegant prostitutes, Carol and Kathy, who became Bernardo's roommates up in Laurel Canyon. These gals were stylish, super-hip hookers, the sort that hustled on Sunset Boulevard in velvet 1940s opera gowns that they'd scissor-slashed into fashionable micro-mini-dresses. There was also a tall Texan named Connie Gripp—also known as Chi Chi Connie, the notorious groupie and future girlfriend of Dee Dee Ramone, from *Please Kill Me*—who would later become my lover and one of my best gal pals.

I wouldn't say Connie was a female love of my life; I didn't pine for her the way I did for Sapphire. One night we got really loaded on Seconal and did have sex, but I don't remember much about the encounter because, well, I was on drugs. I was always on drugs. When *wasn't* I on drugs? Anyway, that was a one-time tryst, but Connie and I remained very close, and we were like a couple—it was a partnership kind of deal.

Connie might have been a prostitute, a heroin addict, and prone to freaky fits of out-of-the-blue violence, but she was amazingly fun and had a heart full of fool's gold. We always looked out for each other. One night Connie went out to turn a trick, and that little voice echoed in my head again. I warned her, "Don't go out. There's danger waiting for you!" She went out anyway, and when she returned, she told me she'd almost been stabbed to death. I was so relieved she was okay. She listened to me from that point on.

One of my first celebrity-sighting adventures upon landing in LA occurred when Connie and I were hitchhiking down Sunset, and as our ride pulled up to the stoplight, there was the Jackson 5's tour bus, purring right beside us. We excitedly waved to them, and little Michael Jackson, who couldn't have been older than ten, leaned out the window and cheerfully yelled, "Follow us!" He was hardly the shy, timid little mouse he became as an adult. So we ordered our driver to trail after the bus, and we ended up in some school cafeteria, which the Jacksons were using as a practice space. Connie and I had only begun to marvel at this phenomenally talented kid and his funky brothers in action when their dadager, the disreputable Joe Jackson, kicked us out. Joe claimed this was because the boys, particularly Michael, were total perfectionists and their routine wasn't ready for public viewing. But I am sure it's because we looked like freaks, even by Hollyweird standards—me dressed like the wicked witch from *The Wiz*, Connie decked out in her happy-hooker threads. To this day, I wonder if Michael got the idea for all his *Bad* belts from me.

And finally, in that aforementioned Laurel Canyon house lived the lovely Christine Frka, a pale vision with her handmade dolly frocks and headful of uncontrollable madwoman ringlets. Christine and I also became soul sisters. When I met her, I thought, "This chick is a lot like me, only she's skinny." To be honest, Christine and I mainly connected over our shared need for speed, but I liked her straight away. She was exquisitely beautiful, she was strange, and she was utterly unique, like a Dr. Seuss character. Christine was definitely not a prostitute—that was the furthest thing from her mind, *trust me*. Instead of hooking and hustling, Christine got a day job as the avant-garde genius musician Frank Zappa's nanny and housekeeper, often secretly shooting methamphetamine to power through her domestic duties. Eventually she moved over to the Zappa family's Laurel Canyon homestead, the Log Cabin, down the street.

Next door to the Log Cabin lived Vito Paulekas, an eccentric older artist who chased younger chicks. I didn't know very much about him, but his whole vibe frightened the hell out of me. He was like eighty! That's how old he seemed to me, anyway. But I knew Vito was a big deal, and his house was the ultimate LA hangout in the sixties. Anybody who was anybody was there, from Sal Mineo to Bobby Beausoleil, and everybody wanted to be there. Everyone was dancing, flipping out, tripping out. Sex antics and orgies were going on in every corner. To loosely quote Rick James, it was such a freaky scene. It wasn't *my* scene, really, but that's how I got into dancing with the Laurel Canyon Ballet Company, the prototype for the GTOs.

I first met Pamela Des Barres, then known as Pamela Miller, dancing at Vito's place. I can't figure it out, but we had some kind of instant connection. She and I could not have been more opposite. I was a heavyset, dark-eyed witch dressed in rags, and she was an innocent, sparkling flower, this pretty, peppy little sexpot of a girl. I was abrasive and tough, and she was sugar 'n' spice and everything nice. She didn't really do drugs—I mean, she'd do the occasional line of cocaine or hit of acid, but she was never a shooter like I was—and she'd had a sheltered upbringing, with two parents that were at home and actually cared about what she did. Pamela was wild in her own way, definitely much more sexually driven than I ever was, but she was relatively normal.

Pamela had never met anyone like me. I know I overwhelmed her and scared the fuck out of her. She just wasn't ready for me. I admit it, I was pretty scary. I was aware that I had that effect on people, but it didn't concern me that I was intimidating. That just made me want to be *more* intimidating. I *liked* being that way. Pamela later wrote in her memoir *I'm with the Band* that I seemed like a "threat to normalcy." I almost made that the title of this book. That's a compliment, as far as I'm concerned.

But somehow, Pamela and I took to each other and became best friends. Pamela always accepted me for the way I was, even when I lost my mind and was at my craziest. Without her, my life would

Mercy Fontenot *and* Lyndsey Parker

be entirely different today. A psychic once told Pamela that in a previous life, I was her mother and we lived in Hollywood, and that I abandoned her to be a movie star but I didn't make it. Sounds about right. Our friendship goes back many lifetimes, supposedly. Maybe this is our last life together, or maybe there will be more. We shall see.

The Laurel Canyon Ballet Company had already formed with Christine, Pamela, Pamela's childhood friend Sparky, and two other scenester girls, Lucy and Sandra, when Frank Zappa came up with a much more ambitious vision for the girls: an experimental band of groupies called the GTOs. It was around that time that I paid Christine a visit at the Log Cabin. I brought with me another new gal pal of mine, Cynderella, a skinny rich chick who wasn't very into eating but was definitely into shooting junk. Cynderella was nutty as a fruitcake and a ton of fun. Frank took one look at the two of us and proclaimed, "Put them in this group, *now*! We must add Mercy and Cynderella to be more diverse." I suspect he really meant more *perverse*. He had already formed the GTOs, but he thought there was an element missing, a certain freakiness. Cynderella and I certainly had that to offer, if nothing else.

And just like that, suddenly I was in the GTOs, a.k.a. the aptly named Girls Together Outrageously. I didn't have to be talked into it. Once you got into Frank's world, you were at his command. "Okay. I'll do this. It'll be a gas." Cynderella's then-boyfriend Tiny Tim gave us our "Miss" titles, which seemed to make it all official, and we became the GTOs and inked our Straight Records contracts. We were going to be rock stars, just like the people we idolized.

I admit that the first time I met Frank, I wasn't very impressed. I didn't respect the Mothers of Invention, or at least what I thought the media had painted them out to be. I thought Frank was nice but a bit of dingbat, and that his music was gimmicky and silly. But I soon recognized his brilliance, starting with when he gave me a Smokey

Robinson & the Miracles record and I realized he was into soul music too. One of the first times I recall being awed by Frank was when I wandered into one of his sessions and this cute Black guy was playing rock 'n' roll violin. I said, "Who the heck is this?" It was Sugarcane Harris. I was floored. I had no idea what Frank had going on, how many people he was working with. To watch Frank record, in any kind of session, was just something else. Eventually I grew to adore him. Frank changed my life by putting me in the GTOs, and for that I will be eternally grateful. I really miss him.

❧

AFTER I RAN AWAY FROM the authorities, my mother eventually showed up in Los Angeles. I would accuse her of following me, but she said she was simply "supporting" me. I suppose she was. Later in life, I was glad she was there. My dad followed me down to LA too. That I was less thrilled about. I'm sure my father had no idea what was happening, but my mother thought it was pretty cool. She went to Frank's house with me once. She thought the scene was kind of bizarre, but the Turtles were there that day, so that impressed her.

The GTOs were a "girl group," but were hardly some manufactured creation, and Zappa was not our Svengali. We styled ourselves; there was no Hollywood stylist. We dressed the way we wanted to dress, as *us*. Frank told the press, "I picked these girls because they were the way that they were. These girls were their own creation that I needed to put out, that needed to be seen. They need to be historically known." And when it came to material for our one album, he left us to our own devices, for the most part. He told us, "You guys have to do an album now. Write two songs each." And he gave us a deadline and sent us on our merry way.

I came up with the GTOs' album title, *Permanent Damage*. I was at this big dining room table up in Laurel Canyon at my boyfriend

Jobriath's house, and suddenly I announced out loud, *"Permanent Damage!* That's the name of our new album. I just know it!" Then I rang up Frank and he said, "That's a great title." That's how it happened, simple as that. I know the title sounds negative, when the album was actually rather jolly. But being permanently damaged is what created our craziness—and our album was screwy. Let's face it, we were all permanently damaged. We all had stuff in our life to make us the way we were—independent, wacky soloists.

Frank gave us total creative license; much of the time the GTOs rehearsed, he wasn't even there. He just said, "Go do your song, get it done, and then we'll cut it." My first songwriting attempt was "The Ghost Chained to the Past, Present, and Future (Shock Treatment)," inspired by that bizarro time I witnessed Keith Richards get electrocuted onstage in Sacramento. I came up with the melody while hanging out with Keith and Mick Jagger at Sunset Sound, and I ran outside and stood on the street corner while I worked the melody out in my head. *"I see all the people I want to see, I be all the people I want to be,"* I sang. It was a line—a slogan, a mission statement, almost—that summarized my life until that point. Later I got together with Cynderella, humming the tune while she wrote down the chords because she played piano; that's why we both have writing credits on it.

Frank recruited the best of the best in the West for the *Permanent Damage* sessions. We had Jeff Beck on guitar, Nicky Hopkins (famous piano player for the Stones, the Kinks, the Who, everyone) on keyboards, Aynsley Dunbar on drums. But I thought we were doing some silly shit in the studio, if I'm being honest. We were cutting Christine's track, "Eureka Springs Garbage Lady," and Christine could not sing worth a damn. It was downright embarrassing. And here came in Jeff Beck with the *wah-wah* guitar, and I was looking at Frank, going, "Excuse me, but you have one of the greatest guitar players around, and you're putting him on *this* stupid little novelty song? What in the hell are you doing?"

Frank countered, "What do you *want* him to play on, Mercy? On *your* song?" And I said yes, of course.

Rod Stewart just happened to be in Jeff Beck's group, and he just happened to be tagging along at Frank's that day. Rod wasn't a superstar yet, except in his own mind, and he wasn't a session cat like Jeff and Nicky, so he was not hired to sing on my "Shock Treatment" session. None of us had heard him sing yet, so Rod got all flustered and pissed off that nobody knew who he was or was paying any attention to him. Rod was always the most conceited person, extremely ego-driven, though I learned later that deep down he was actually a sweetheart.

Rod was throwing a toddler-style tantrum over being left out of the all-star proceedings, acting like a full-on spoiled brat. I thought he was being terribly obnoxious and that his ego was way too big—especially at this early stage of his career—so I flat-out told him, "You know, nobody's even heard of you yet. The only reason people are coming to see you is because of Jeff Beck." That predictably sent Rod into a rage, and he ran off. Pamela chased after him, took him into the other room, and made him satisfied, so to speak, so he would calm down and just shut the fuck up. But he was still whining and complaining, so finally I blurted out, exasperated, "Jesus Christ, just let this guy sing already!" I honestly only wanted to appease Rod so he'd calm down. But once he opened his mouth, I was amazed.

I started singing "Shock Treatment," and then Rod came in, ad-libbing over and over, "*Shock treatment, oh, oh, please let me gooooo.*" I immediately backed away from the microphone and told Frank, "You know what? Just let Rod sing the rest of this. Forget my lyrics. This guy's voice is incredible!" That track ended up being all about Rod, which I am sure made him happy. But I didn't even mind because I was always about promoting, discovering, and encouraging true talent, and I knew this guy was special. Rod may have had a gigantic ego, but I couldn't blame him once I heard him sing.

"Shock Treatment" is actually on some Rod Stewart compilation album. I'm supposed to be getting some money from somewhere, but I never got it. I still don't know where the residuals are. I want my money.

Rod—or "Rodney the Rooster," as I used to call him—and I became buddies after that and got up to all sorts of LA adventures. He was a man of style but very broke, so we'd hitchhike to the Glass Farm House vintage clothing emporium in Silver Lake to score our threads for cheap. On Thanksgiving, he had no food, so he came over for a makeshift feast at the Landmark Hotel (the same place where Janis Joplin would die a couple years later) where Frank had rented a room for me, Christine, and Cynderella. The Landmark had a revolving rotation of entertainers—Alice Cooper and his manager, Shep Gordon; Earth, Wind & Fire; Willie Chambers of the Chambers Brothers; Ten Years After. Everybody lived there. I spent the night there with Rod on Thanksgiving, in the same twin bed, but I did not *sleep* with him, if you know what I mean. All night, Rod kept playing the record "Please Return Your Love to Me" by David Ruffin, over and over and over. He was a big soul freak, so that was cool.

My other contribution to the *Permanent Damage* album was "I Have a Paintbrush in My Hand to Color a Triangle," which was about an imagined love triangle between me, Bernardo Saldana, and Brian Jones. The "boy with dark skin" with "eyes of hot coals" was Bernardo, a.k.a. "Scarlet," and the "boy with ivory skin, eyes of sea green, hair of pale gold" was Brian, a.k.a. "Marigold." That "changing lovers into orphans" line haunts me now that both Brian and Bernardo are gone. Frank had recruited Lowell George from Little Feat for the GTOs album, and I would go over to Lowell's house to rehearse this song, just the two of us, with him playing the piano while I hummed the melody to him, since I didn't write or play music. I felt Lowell was very respectful as a collaborator. Decades later, I heard his unreleased demo of our song on YouTube, and it blew me away. I never knew that demo existed until a couple years ago.

I won't go so far as to say that rock legends like Jeff Beck and Lowell George took me 100 percent seriously as an artist or saw me or any of the GTOs as being on equal footing with them. Frank was their friend, plus he was paying them to be on the GTOs sessions. I seriously doubt they thought, "Wow, this is real talent!" But I think my two songs were pretty good for not knowing anything. They were actual *songs*, while many of the other girls' tracks were more like spoken-word vignettes or comedy skits. Zappa's label even tried to release "Shock Treatment" as a single in England. And many years later, I was flipping TV channels and I landed on Morton Downey Jr.'s show and saw an all-girl metal group called Cycle Sluts From Hell performing "Shock Treatment." My jaw dropped. I was really proud.

I know there were some people who saw the GTOs as a novelty act or a gimmick, and I can understand why. One of the guys in Frank Zappa's band, the Mothers of Invention, said we couldn't put a right note in a bucket, or something like that. I don't see how anyone could think the album was going to be a success, but I think it has held up. It garnered decent reviews at the time. Rock critics didn't say, "This is a piece of shit," so, hey, at least there was that.

The best thing about being in the GTOs was it made us equal to the rock stars that we were hanging with. We wanted to be one of the boys and be *with* the boys, be with the band and be *in* the band, and all our wishes were fulfilled. Through word of mouth we became stars in our own right, especially in England. For the British rock stars, like the guys in Zeppelin and the Stones, it became a rite of passage for them to meet us—or sleep with us—when they swung through Los

Angeles. All those men talked. We were gossip girls. But overall, I feel we had good reputations within the rock scene. We weren't some lowly groupies that would get used and cast aside. And I think doing an album really helped change that perception. "We could say, 'Hey, we are a band now. We're performers and artists, too.'"

The term "groupie" has become derogatory because of the breed of groupies that emerged around the 1980s, the girls who would sleep with just about anybody, who'd suck off a roadie or security guard or tour manager or bus driver just to gain access to the real superstar backstage. They were not as intelligent or musically curious, I think, as we were. They didn't know what was important about the music, where it was recorded, or who wrote it. They had no knowledge of anything except that the guy playing the instrument was famous and cute. That's the negative connotation nowadays, implying that groupies are the lowest on the rock 'n' roll totem pole. But this wasn't the case in my day. The groupies back then didn't just glom onto musicians who were already famous. We were a *part* of the fame. We evangelized and helped make the fame happen. We met these people because we were supposed to.

I never minded being called a groupie, although I didn't set out to be one, and I wouldn't say I ever really was one. At Zappa's Log Cabin, the GTOs had a wall on which we scrawled the names of people we wanted to be with, but for me that didn't necessarily mean physically go to bed with—it just meant people I was going to *get* to. I did sleep with some famous people, but the music was my main thing, just being around musicians, and I wouldn't go to bed with someone because he was famous. It was never about that. I met most of my names on the wall (including my future husband, Shuggie Otis), though I never did get to cross Leonard Cohen, Lenny Bruce, or Tennessee Williams off the list.

Rolling Stone adored the GTOs. Anything we did, they wrote about. I was actually probably written about more than any of the others, even Pamela, at that point, because I was the loudest and weirdest and always getting arrested. I think they reported I died, though obviously I didn't. Hopefully when I really do, *Rolling Stone* will still write about it.

When we were shooting with Baron Wolman for the *Rolling Stone* at A&M studios—this was about a year after Baron had discovered me in Golden Gate Park and put me on the magazine's cover—we were loitering outside with Pauline Butcher, our "nanny," and George Harrison was in the parking lot. Pauline dragged us over to meet him. She didn't have to drag Pamela, of course. Pauline asked George, "Have you heard of the GTOs?" He looked us up and down and said, "Yeah, I've heard a lot about them...and now I *believe* it!"

That Baron Wolman photoshoot at A&M led to me being on *Rolling Stone*'s back cover, on which I was declared one of their "favorite girls of 1969." I was so excited until I unfurled this huge gatefold picture, and there was my nipple showing. I had no idea that I'd been wearing a see-through blouse! Trust me, I was not trying to be sexy.

I honestly don't think the GTOs' appeal, or our reputation, was about the sex thing, other than maybe for Pamela. We weren't just after men; there was a female bond as well. It was a women's movement, and at the end of the day, we had each other's backs. We were having adventures together. Almost all of us were bisexual, though we weren't having sex with each other. I know there were rumors of that, the whole scandalous notion that we were "Together Outrageously" or even "Together Orally"—and we *loved* to push that and let people think what they wanted. We'd walk around holding hands in public; we thought it was cool to be girl-on-girl. It merely added to the fun, but I suppose it was revolutionary for the time.

The GTOs were asked to be on *The Dating Game* once. That was a goofy experience. We went in for our audition, and we had to suggest what we'd ask the bachelor contestants if we were the swinging bachelorettes doing the picking. We proposed questions that were scandalous, but not politically incorrect, for the time, like, "What would you do if you were out on a date with a girl and found out 'she' was a *he*?" We weren't trying to get on the show, really; we thought it was totally square. So the producers said, "Yeah, okay, we don't think we need you after all."

Of all the GTOs, men usually wanted to date Miss Pamela and Miss Christine because they were so adorable. But our diehard fans were mostly female. The GTOs were kind of an early Spice Girls, and every fan had a favorite GTO. I must have been Scary Spice, looking how I did. Only recently did it dawn on me that I, being the chubby one, may have been a role model for bigger girls. Even though I may not have had the fashion-model looks, I was hanging with rock stars and I was on the cover of *Rolling Stone*, and I was an "it" girl. So I may have been the GTO that a lot of regular women could relate to the most.

Sometimes I look at old GTOs photos and my first reaction is, "Oh, my God, I look so fat! Look at how much more beautiful the other girls were," with their Twiggy figures. But then I think maybe it was a good thing that I represented the larger ladies. Maybe it did some good for somebody else, that they could look at me and realize that you can be chunky and weird and yourself and still be in a band and get guys. I never seemed like I was apologizing for my size or trying to hide. Although, to be honest, it was probably difficult to tell how big I actually was under all my layers of Gypsy garments.

What's interesting is even though I was known for being a groupie and therefore sexually free, my clothes were not risqué. I definitely covered up. I wasn't particularly feminine. That wasn't part of my thing. But there were some guys who liked my style. Actually, there were many guys who *copied* my style! Then again, I wasn't necessarily dressing for men's approval. Pamela played the sex kitten and would wear these little teeny things that showed off her gazelle-like gams, but I didn't think that flaunting my cellulite was very sexy. I was more artsy, bohemian, freakish. Modern-day groupies probably wouldn't attract rock stars dressing like that because now you have to look a porn star.

I do recall one time when I tried to pursue Van Morrison and it backfired big-time. I thought he'd adore me because I was so Gypsy-looking, like a character out of one of his colorful story-songs. So I went to the Troubadour wearing three hoop skirts, four belts, bracelets stacked to my armpits, rags wrapped around my head. But when Van opened his dressing room door and got an eyeful of my getup, he got spooked and slammed the door smack in my face. That was depressing.

I was accepted by men in the scene when I was heavier because I was a GTO, but not really as a sex object or as somebody that most men wanted to be with. Had I been skinnier at that time, Lord knows what would have happened. Being as heavy as I was, and so outrageous—you could even say obnoxious—I probably limited my romantic options. Eventually I did shed the weight. I don't have a big secret about how I did it. It's not like I went on Weight Watchers. I just went on speed. And the pounds fell off.

I know I don't get talked about like other famous groupies, like Bebe Buell, or Sable Starr, or especially Pamela. I'm never in any "Top 10 Groupies" list. But I was confident. I was really funny and real fun. I became a comedy character, because I had to be. I made people roll over laughing. I was fucking *funny*. I knew I wasn't really beautiful, but beauty isn't everything; if you put a bunch of pretty girls in a lineup, they all become beautiful and pretty soon you can't tell one from the other. So I still had confidence, most of the time—not necessarily in my looks, but I believed I had a certain magic in me.

Mercy Fontenot *and* Lyndsey Parker

People thought the GTOs' image was all about not giving a fuck. It actually was all about *giving* a fuck. We went out of our way to make scenes. We'd make a plan and say, "We're going to show up at the Whisky together." And then we'd go straight to the booth with the most famous people at the club and sit down next to them, or on top of them. They already knew us. But we weren't real performers yet, and eventually it was time for us to be onstage, not backstage. Our big live concert debut would take place in December 1968 at the Shrine Auditorium, opening for the Mothers of Invention, Alice Cooper, and Wild Man Fischer.

This was a big fucking deal. We rehearsed for two months at the Lindy Opera House, right next door to Linda Ronstadt and the Stone Poneys. We were a very united front and took it all dead seriously. Sure, Christine, Cynderella, and I shot speed before every rehearsal, but that didn't affect our ability to perform—if anything, it enhanced us and made everything easier. Pauline walked in on us in the restroom a couple times and asked what we were up to, but it was easy to deceive her. She'd pop in all cheerily and say, "'Ello, girls, are you ready to go on yet?" Pauline was completely oblivious, naive as hell, very English, very proper, and very unqualified. Her job was to take care of the GTOs, drive us around, chaperone us, keep us out of trouble—make sure we were at our appointments, paying our rent, stuff like that. But if part of her job was to keep us off drugs, she clearly failed in that mission.

We were all pumped up and feeling confident the night of the show until our pal Gram Parsons showed up with his fellow Flying Burrito Brother Chris Hillman and Oscar-nominated actor Brandon deWilde, and they whisked Pamela and me off for a ride in Gram's T-Bird. Then they got us really, really, really loaded on pot. I mean, Gram did not fuck around—he only smoked the best of the best. When we rolled back up to the Shrine, Christine was frantic, hissing at me, "If you fuck this up, Mercy, *I will kill you.*" I don't remember much about that night, but I will never forget the look of pure fury on her face.

I do remember we were excellent that night. Christine's threat got my head right. It was good that she'd said that, otherwise I might have been flying high and not able to even find the stage. The show at the Shrine had a lot of dialogue; it was much more like Cockettes-esque performance art than a regular concert, with bizarre theater pieces leading into each song. There was a skit with us shopping and looking through bras and throwing them up in the air, burlesque sequences, Rodney Bingenheimer playing Santa Claus. It wasn't some sloppy amateur hour, which a lot of people who weren't there might assume. Every moment of that show was meticulously choreographed and scripted, and after what felt like 10,000 hours of rehearsing, we had it *down*. Nothing was going to screw this up for us, not even Gram's weed. We nailed all our lines and did everything we were supposed to, and for the grand finale we were all paired off for a dance contest. Miss Sandra and I did the tango, and we totally killed it.

By the time our album came out a year later, the GTOs were basically over.

There was a lot of hype surrounding the GTOs. Frank's label was really going to push us—until we got into trouble. I got arrested, Christine got arrested, and Frank called the whole thing off. He wanted nothing to do with us. Let me make this very clear: Frank Zappa had no idea what Christine, Cynderella, and I were up to. He would not have tolerated it. When it came to drugs, Frank was extremely straight.

A typical day for Christine, Cynderella, and me back then was spent searching for speed, because speed was tremendously difficult to find in LA compared to the meth haven that had been San Francisco. Pamela wasn't very cool about all this. Once she came to visit us at the Landmark and walked in on us shooting up, and she fled back to her car and sobbed. I chased after her and assured her, "Oh, please don't cry, Pamela, darling. It's all right. We'll be fine." We were not fine.

After leaving the Landmark, Christine and I moved into this quaint little bungalow on Highland Avenue for a while, and that's when she started to go crazy from meth, picking bugs out of her skin. She and I went out one night to score drugs—speed for her, morphine for me—and that was when I met Chuck Wein, a Warhol associate who did the Edie Sedgwick film *Ciao Manhattan!* and later Jimi Hendrix's *Rainbow Bridge*. We were winding our way through Laurel Canyon to see Jobriath, but he wasn't home. And then on the way down, we got pulled over. The cops claimed they were stopping us because of a burglary in the area, but that was a bunch of bullshit, of course.

I am a conspiracy theorist by nature, so I always thought the authorities were out to get us. Christine had told me a story that she was in our apartment shooting up by the window and some cops were driving through the alley, saw her, and came pounding at our door and busted in. But they couldn't find anything, so they didn't arrest her at that time. I believe LAPD was on a mission to catch us from that point on, but I have no real proof of that. Just another one of my premonitions.

My purse that night in Laurel Canyon was packed with syringes and morphine, so I tossed it under the backseat. Unfortunately, I wasn't very smooth about it, and the cops totally witnessed me doing this. Deep down, though, I think I *wanted* to get caught, because I really didn't want to be a morphine addict, and I thought getting arrested would maybe help me kick the habit. Christine was more successful in stashing her speed, so the police didn't nab her even though they took her to the station for questioning for like a minute. One of the cops had a big crush on her, so he let her go almost immediately. She got back in the car, opened a book, and there was the speed she'd left.

Regarding the charges against me, the public defender took me into a room and explained, "We're not going to charge you with possession of morphine. We're going to change it to heroin"—which, oddly, at that time was a lesser offense—"so you won't have to do time." I was in jail for three whole weeks before I got out. When I finally made it to the courtroom, both my parents were there, and Jobriath had sent Christine with some money. But Christine had spent the money, so my parents ultimately had to bail me out. I got convicted of possession of a controlled substance and paraphernalia—syringes—and I was placed on probation.

Despite my reduced charges, Frank had zero desire to be affiliated with drug users, period, so he fired all of the GTOs—canceled everything, cut off our allowances. It was over. The album was about to come out, so we put up a unified front to the public for a while, but it was a done deal. I couldn't even fly with Pamela to London to promote the album because I was on probation. I had ruined it for everyone. I'm sorry.

The GTOs all went our separate ways. We didn't necessarily go on to have the most conventional lifestyles, but at the end of the day, I suppose we all had the normal, traditional goal of getting married and starting families—the same thing most women wanted. The difference was we wanted to marry rock stars, and some of us did. Pamela married Michael Des Barres, Cynderella was married to John Cale from the Velvet Underground for a bit, and I got with Shuggie Otis. Christine definitely would have married a rock star if she had lived. Even she would have eventually settled down.

Most of the GTOs are very dead now. Miss Lucy died of AIDS in 1991; Miss Sandra died of cancer that same year. Cynderella passed

Mercy Fontenot *and* Lyndsey Parker

away sometime in the late nineties under mysterious circumstances. Christine supposedly died by suicide. She had very bad scoliosis and went to England to have back surgery; she spent about a year in a body cast, and when she came back, she was like a completely different person. She later died in Jonathan Richman's house—she'd been dating David Robinson, the drummer for Jonathan's band, the Modern Lovers—and I still have no idea what really happened. I don't like to think about it.

Shortly after Christine returned from the UK, she came over to visit me when I was writing a script for what was supposed to be the GTOs' comeback or reunion show of sorts at the Hollywood Palladium, "Hollywood Babylon," in which were going to play whores from Spanish Harlem. Iggy Pop and the Cockettes were also supposed to be on the bill; there were posters made and everything, and it was going to be amazing, historic. But Christine seemed changed. Our bond was severed and our friendship was clearly over. She told me I couldn't pay her enough to sign on for this project. She read the dialogue I'd written, threw the script to the floor, and screamed, "This is trash!" Then she took off in a huff. So I recruited Connie Gripp as a substitute/honorary GTO, but then the show got canceled anyway. And that was the last time I saw Christine.

The only event that came close to a real GTOs reunion was a show on October 11, 1974, also at the Palladium, called the "Hollywood Street Revival," at which Cynderella, Sparky, Pamela, another honorary GTO named Geraldine, and I were the opening act for Pamela's new boyfriend Michael Des Barres and his glam band Silverhead; Iggy Pop, Flo & Eddie, and the New York Dolls were also on the bill. I suggested we sing "Mr. Sandman," but then I pulled out of the gig because I was serious with my future husband, Shuggie Otis, by then; he was irrationally possessive and jealous, and I knew he would not approve. Shuggie thought it wasn't proper for me to be in the GTOs. He objected to most activities that would entail me fraternizing outside the house with other musicians.

But then, on the day of the show, Cynderella called me up and convinced me to do it after all. The other girls had been rehearsing diligently, but she assured me it would be fine for us to just show up out of nowhere (apparently she'd skipped out on rehearsals as well). I told Shuggie, "Cynderella and I are going to the pictures, see you later!" Shuggie asked if he could come too, but I told him, "No, no, you should stay home; it's a girls' night out, just her and I." Somehow he believed I was going to the movies when I was all dressed up like a prostitute, with a big black Ronnie Spector wig and teeny cinched waist. I looked fucking fabulous, by the way.

Unfortunately, when Cynderella came by to pick me up, she had this china white heroin from France, so we got blitzed out of our gourds. We walked into the venue just as the GTOs were about to go on and said all brightly and casually, "Hey, guys, we're here!" Sparky and Pamela weren't too thrilled to see us, especially when I became sick as a dog from the smack and started throwing up backstage. Johnny Thunders and Iggy Pop were milling about, and there I was behaving worse than those notorious junkies, vomiting everywhere, sticking my head in garbage cans. Somehow I made it to the stage and powered through "Mr. Sandman," and we were going to perform "Jailhouse Rock" with Michael, but then I stumbled into the stage wings and hurled some more.

Later, when I got home, Shuggie eagerly sniffed up the rest of the French heroin, but not before his father, the legendary bandleader Johnny Otis, pounced on me the minute I stepped through the door. "How could you do that to the family?" he screamed.

I said, "What on earth are you talking about? Do *what*?"

Johnny said, "I saw you on the TV. How could you embarrass us like that?" I had no idea that this Palladium concert was a splashy event that was going to be on the evening news. There would be no more GTOs reunion attempts after that.

I still to this day don't know what the grand vision was for the GTOs. To me, we were just having fun and doing whatever we felt like doing. We didn't consider ourselves "feminist"—I don't even remember that word being used to describe us—because that label had a different connotation at the time. We were all pursuing men; we loved men. Now, I realize that you can consider yourself a feminist and still like men, but the public perception was different then.

However, I am proud that we were one of the first female groups to break through the barriers. We hung with rock stars on their turf, and it was *our* turf, too. We weren't the first groupies—that had been going on for years—but groupies weren't talked about before us. The topic was taboo; the record labels probably didn't want any affairs out in the open out of fear it might hurt the artists' careers. So the GTOs shattered that stigma to some degree—I mean, we were in a *Rolling Stone* "Groupie Issue," proudly identifying as such. And we probably promoted lesbianism even though that wasn't necessarily our agenda.

Later, when I got involved in the LA punk scene, I could see the line between the GTOs and punk—because the ethos of punk was that you didn't have to be a professional musician or be trained to play and read music. You could do it yourself. You could be someone who's never even picked up an instrument before and start a band. The GTOs were like that. I guess we were punk-rock in our own way.

4

Take Me I'm Yours

ONE NIGHT WHEN I WAS still a GTO, Christine and I went to see a production of *Hair* at the Aquarius Theater on Sunset. *Hair* was the place to be, a hot ticket; I recall the future Bianca Jagger was in the audience. This was where I met another one of the great loves of my life, Jobriath, who played the second lead, Woof. I vividly remember gazing up at him in the spotlight, this pretty hippie-dippie angel-boy, and thinking in that moment, "I'm going to go up on that stage, and I will never go home again." And then he came and got me. Maybe he heard me; maybe he'd read my mind. Or maybe, once again, I had willed a dream into reality.

At the end of every *Hair* performance, it was a tradition to bring an audience member onstage. I was sitting in the aisle seat and felt this compulsion to run up there, but I was too afraid to volunteer. But then suddenly, I was telling Christine, "This guy is coming straight at me!" Jobriath dragged me from my seat, and from that moment on, he and I became inseparable. It was an instantaneous connection. *Something* happened; I think Cupid flew over. I was under Jobriath's spell, he was under mine, and we were simply *together*. I went home with him that night, and we became an item of sorts for about the next two years. I was just nuts over him, absolutely crazy over him.

Jobriath whisked me off to this sprawling, lavish house up in Laurel Canyon, where he lived with some very gay guy and some young actor and another much older man, and I watched him play his glossy grand piano. At the time, he was in the folk-rock band Pidgeon, who put out one decent album on Decca Records, but that project hardly showcased his true genius. This man could *play*: I sat there at his side, enraptured, as he performed compositions by Stravinsky, Mozart, Debussy, and Beethoven, sounding like all of them put together. I could listen to Jobriath play piano for hours. I was convinced that he was a vessel, possessed by all these classical greats of the past, all of these resurrected composers coming through him. I still believe that.

Most people never knew that side of Jobriath, or even knew of him at all. He's now mainly remembered as one of rock 'n' roll's most tragic cautionary tales. In the early seventies, he was touted as the "American David Bowie," with this massive marketing blitz led by the infamous and obnoxious impresario Jerry Brandt, but the backlash to all that hype, by both the public and critics, was swift and vicious, and he later died in obscurity, disgraced. Much of that backlash probably had to do with the fact that he was openly gay and declared himself "the true fairy of rock 'n' roll." But I met him before his whole glam trip. I think he was better than that, and that he deserved better.

Yes, I fell deeply in love with Jobriath, and he did fall in love with me—even though he was gay. I didn't realize that at first. He didn't act like the flamboyant "fairy" stereotype he ended up becoming, the guy who captured Morrissey's attention and inspired Todd Haynes's glam-rock cinematic fable *Velvet Goldmine*. It's not like he was running around being all sassy, announcing, "Hey, I'm gay!" and snapping his fingers. Sure, we'd go to gay clubs, but who didn't? Half of my boyfriends wore dresses back then, anyway. Men liking men, men dressing as women, that was all common where I was from—in San Francisco and Hollywood, it was no big thing.

I finally got wise when Sal Mineo came over to our place one night to pick Jobriath up for a date, wearing these spectacular thigh-high boots. Honestly, that was fine with me; Sal was so gorgeous, I couldn't blame *anyone* for wanting to go on a date with him. But there was no grandiose coming-out speech from Jobriath, no heart-to-heart chat. I just figured it out and accepted it. I must've known deep down because even though he and I slept in the same bed and held hands and all that, our relationship was clearly not going anywhere. I was disappointed at first, but the platonic-ness of it all was ultimately fine by me. I never tried to push it in another direction because I was simply in awe to be around this man. There are some people, like Jobriath or Bernardo or Sapphire, who are just above the law, and to consummate the relationship would probably only mess it up. Then they'd become just another "somebody I slept with."

If anything, Jobriath's homosexuality made him even more attractive to me. I thought it was fabulous. People used to call me a "fag hag," and I know that's not a politically correct term, but I was proud to be a fag hag. I'd hung out in gay clubs in San Francisco because they had the best music and the best dancing, and I always ended up having crushes on these pretty boys. That was my type. You know that Eagles song, "she got a lot of pretty, pretty boys that she calls friends"? That was totally me. Sometimes my fantasy was to turn these boys straight, of course. I know it sounds foolish now, but I saw it as more of a pansexual thing, or a try-sexual thing…and I wanted these guys to give me a try! Did I ever convert them? Hell, no. I did have sex with a few, but they were bi. Jobriath was beyond "conversion."

Dating a gay man was like having a girlfriend and a boyfriend at the same time. So that was fun, except when they stole my clothes—

then I'd get really pissed! I dated Reggie from San Francisco's avant-garde, gender-bending theater troupe the Cockettes for a while. He was tall, slim, androgynous—beautiful like a woman and handsome like a man. The Cockettes were a ton of fun. We were around each other a lot so we rubbed off on each other, style-wise. I didn't find them attractive with their beards, but Reggie was my boyfriend for a while and we did go to bed together. Mostly, though, we were just dear friends.

I was simply attracted to beautiful people, as we all are. I never was into labels and identity politics. It didn't dawn on me to ask, "Are you gay? Are you straight? Are you bi? Are you trans? Are you feminist? Are you this? Are you that?" Everybody just got along and didn't put labels on everybody. I'd always felt like I was in between genders myself. I always had a lot of masculine qualities, as well as a lot of feminine ones. I didn't identify with being a woman, nor did I identify with being a man. Sometimes after I took a hit of acid I even felt like a boy, like a little Charles Dickens boy. I guess I consider myself bisexual. I was actually more physically attracted to women, really, even though I had very few actual romances with them. If I had my life to do over, I definitely would have chased some women down.

The first girl I ever had a crush on was when I was about eight. It was Halloween, and in the school play I played a lion and she was the Queen of Hearts. She looked like a living doll in that costume. That's the first time I recall having feelings for a girl. I think a lot of my girlfriends are almost romantic, in a way. It's like a platonic romance. They're part of my love life. I can't really explain it, other than the love is intense. I guess I have always been more romantically driven than sexually driven.

There was this one woman, Marsha, whom I went to bed with when I was spending the night at *Rainbow Bridge* director Chuck Wein's house. She kind of molested me, just aggressively went after me, and I let her do what she wanted to do. She was kissing me and fondling my breasts and whatever, but I didn't try to stop her because it frankly didn't bother me. Marsha was gorgeous when I slept with her, but years later when she came to visit me, she scared the living fuck out of me because she had aged so much. She was actually younger than me, but she looked about seventy-five years old. After she died, I found out she'd been shooting Ritalin for years. It made her look like a fossilized tree. Or like Keith Richards.

Anyway, Jobriath and I may not have had a physical relationship, but it was an *affair*, believe me. It was a typical puppy-love experience. Everybody knew we were together, and he would get wildly jealous. One time there was this lovely Gypsy girl living across the street from us at a motel, and I went over to visit her. When I came back, Jobriath slapped me across the face and called me a dyke, screaming, "How *dare* you go after that girl? I saw you!"

Another time he slugged me when he and I were out with Jimmy Page at a Bo Diddley concert. I had gone with Jimmy, but not as a date; Jimmy was just a friend of mine, so I am not sure why Jobriath was so furious. I was shocked and ran outside to cry, but it wasn't that huge a deal to me. I'd been beaten up before, much worse, which I'll get into later; this particular blow wasn't even hard enough to leave a mark. When Jimmy came out to check on me and asked what was wrong, I exclaimed through my tears, "I missed the Bo Diddley show!" My priorities were always in the right place, I guess.

Jobriath really was a gentle soul most of the time. But he was a *tortured* soul, and therefore prone to these unexplained fits of rage. For a while he was crashing at Robert Stigwood's house with some cute gay boy while I lived down the block, and that's where I caught him chopping up his precious piano one day. He was completely flipping out, attacking the piano, beating the heck out of it with a hammer, and howling, "I'm possessed! The devil owns me! Satan has

Mercy Fontenot *and* Lyndsey Parker

his hold on me!" I'd always thought he was possessed, off and on, by people like Beethoven and Stravinsky—but I didn't know *what* was coming out of him this day. His roommate and I pounced on him and pinned him down as we tried shake him into submission. It was one of the strangest experiences I ever had because I do believe that some evil spirit came through him that day.

Jobriath did tons of meth, as many stage actors did then, and he had a whole racket lined up with his doctors. His speed thing dated back to his *Hair* days. Once I traveled with Jobriath to New York, and he and the guy who cowrote *Hair*, James Rado, took me to meet Max Jacobson—a.k.a. "Miracle Max" or "Dr. Feelgood," or the inspiration for the Beatles' "Doctor Robert," who had been President Kennedy's doctor. Max had been tied up with all these celebrities— Edie Sedgwick, Lauren Bacall, Marlene Dietrich, Eddie Fisher, Judy Garland, Thelonious Monk, Marilyn Monroe, Elvis Presley, Elizabeth Taylor, Tennessee Williams. Just about anybody who was anybody was on his list of patients. Jobriath's *Hair* castmates were all into injecting themselves with his "vitamin shots"; that's what Broadway was all about.

The first time I knew anything about Max Jacobson was when I was backstage at *Hair* at the Aquarius Theatre and James had a little suitcase full of methamphetamines and shot everyone up so they could get onstage and put on a good show. Max had apparently given James these drugs to take with him from New York. When I went to New York with Jobriath, James said, "Hey, you want to go over to see Max? He's our speed doctor." I said sure, because I kind of wanted to see for myself if this doctor was good or evil.

Because we were paying $200 a shot, the staff treated us very well. The waiting room had all these Wall Street people in their buttoned-up business suits, but we were put ahead of them. Then Max escorted me into his exam room, and I was shocked by how shabby it all was. This did not look like a clinic for an A-list clientele. It looked more like a crime scene, with used syringes scattered on the floor and blood sprayed all over walls that were otherwise decorated mostly with pictures of Max's star client, JFK. The doc asked me what I wanted, and I answered, "I want some speed, I guess." Max proceeded to mix up some concoction he claimed had vitamin B and all these key nutrients in it, but I stopped him and said, "Really, I just want some meth. Nothing fancy." Whatever he shot me up with, it didn't do much. Maybe all the vitamin B toned it down.

Perhaps it speaks volumes about my tolerance level that a shot from the infamous Dr. Feelgood made me feel almost nothing. But I took a second shot that day, this one administered by Max's nurse, and she booted me—what that means is, she shot me up, drew the blood back out through the syringe, and then she shot me again, so it was like shooting up twice, a two-for-one special. That's how crazy this scene was. That rock 'n' roll nurse had holes all over her arms.

I actually loved Max as a person. I had gone out of my way to learn about him, to find out if he was this mad scientist trying to push drugs, and I came to the conclusion that he wasn't. He was a charismatic and entertaining man, but by the time we knew him, he was a pretty strung-out himself. It was sad to see. The DA had almost nabbed him by this point. But he really didn't mean to hurt anybody—that's how I see it, anyway. I believe he actually thought he was doing good.

The second time we visited Max was at his swank NYC apartment—but just like the doctor's office, it really wasn't so swanky on the inside. Everything was torn up, with hardly any furniture or accoutrements except for the photographs of, once again, John F. Kennedy tacked to the walls. Max greeted us all animated and announced, "I have a new formula that's going to help save everybody because I've messed up so badly."

It was some sort of addiction cure-all. He brought in this guy for a live demonstration, and he insisted that his new formula was going to save the world. He confessed that he felt guilt that he had destroyed the world with drugs, that even his daughter was strung-out because of him, and he was really torn up over it. He said, "This is what I get to offer everybody. With this miracle formula, I can save my daughter, I can save everybody. I'm so happy I can help these people whose lives I've destroyed."

The man Max proceeded to demonstrate on looked fit and vibrant and healthy, and he attested, "I have no memory of being an addict! I am cured!"

This guy claimed that Max's magic shot had not only stopped his $500-a-day heroin habit, but had obliterated any memory he had of his smack days. And Max was so proud, shouting, "Look at my new discovery, look at my new discovery, look what I've done!" I certainly was not trying to kick anything, so I wasn't interested in Max's "cure." It all seemed very Jim Jones to me; this guy was drinking some sort of Kool-Aid, that was certain. But I thought it was kind of interesting that Max was so proud of this formula. It made me think, "This guy is all right. He must be a decent person. His intentions are good."

Jobriath and I lost touch for a while when he was doing all that crazy stuff with Jerry Brandt. I had no idea that he had supposedly become this flashy glam-rock star; I didn't know about all the money behind him, the rumored $500,000 Elektra Records contract, the Times Square billboard, etc. I had no idea what his life had become. Things ended with Jobriath because, first and foremost, Shuggie Otis became "The One." But Jobriath was also clearly going down his own path. I didn't care much for his new musical direction. I thought, "What the hell is this noise? What about the classical stuff?" But I later found out that his song "City Freak" was about me. The lyrics went, "My old lady is a city freak / She has gold where her fingers used to be / And she guards her life with a jewel-encrusted rubber knife / And goes to market at Goodwill Industries." Prophetic, huh? I've worked at Goodwill for the last twenty years.

Connie Gripp went after Jobriath after I got through with him. I know this sounds bizarre, but I saw Cupid. I was at the Whisky, and Cupid actually went whizzing by me, a teeny flying cherub, and shot an arrow straight into Connie and Jobriath's hearts. I thought to myself, "Oh, my God, this is the next power couple."

Once when Connie and I were in a limousine with Jobriath, we got in a knock-down, drag-out fight. I don't even know what the fight was about. I wasn't jealous of their relationship or anything like that; I accepted it and believed it was their fate, and I was genuinely happy for them. Besides, I was too smitten with Shuggie by then to care. But I vividly recall leaning out the door, jutting my leg out, and trying to stop the limo with my foot like I was Fred Flintstone. It was ridiculous. As it turned out, jumping out of cars would become a recurring theme in my life.

Years later, I went to visit Jobriath when he was staying with Barry De Prendergast, the producer of *Rainbow Bridge*. I had my son, Lucky, with me. Jobriath was showing me all his diet pills, laid out like precious gemstones in one of those days-of-the-week pillboxes: "This color is for Tuesday, this color is for Wednesday, this color is for Thursday, this color is for Friday..." They were all speed, basically.

I was like, "Okay, okay. Can I have some?" That's when I found out more about Jobriath's secret past.

I remember sipping these little airplane-cart booze shots that he had brought back from a recent flight to New York, and I got kind of drunk, and Jobriath was telling me, "You know, I'm not actually 'Jobriath.' I'm Bruce Campbell, and I'm AWOL from the army, and they're looking for me." I never knew anything about this before.

Mercy Fontenot *and* Lyndsey Parker

That was the last time I really spoke with Jobriath, other than an occasion when Shuggie and I ran into him at the Chateau Marmont. Somebody in his entourage said, "Punk rock has just come to town. Blondie is over at the Wilton Hilton. You want to go over there?"

And I said, "What the hell is punk?" and "Hell, no, I don't want to go!" We didn't even know who Blondie was. So, we didn't go. I wish we had because it probably would've been very amusing. And I would have gotten more time with Jobriath.

I found out Jobriath passed away in 1983. I was at the gas station on Sunset across from the Whisky a Go Go, and the actress Teda Bracci, who had been in *Hair* and was actually Dusty Springfield's last girlfriend, approached me out of nowhere and told me, "Jobriath is dead. He died of AIDS."

I snapped, "What the hell is AIDS? What are you talking about?" And she explained it was some new disease that had come along, which at that time many people believed was a "gay cancer." This was the first time I had heard of "AIDS"; up until a year before, doctors were still calling it GRID, for "gay-related immune deficiency."

I was very saddened, but Jobriath and I had been apart for so long that I can't claim I was destroyed by the news. I felt mostly numb. However, much later in life, when I saw a picture of Jobriath pop up on Pamela's computer screen, I instantly burst into tears. I think I just put the grief behind me, or inside of me, and stored it away somewhere. I have a tendency to do that, I suppose, for self-protection. I just black things out that are going to bother me.

5

Grievous Angel

I NEVER THOUGHT JIMI Hendrix, or Brian Jones, or Jim Morrison, or Janis Joplin were going to last. They were like burning stars; they flared too hard and too fast, like flashes of light or balls of fire. Their energy was too strong. I believe that's what the fates had planned for them, though. I cannot imagine an older Janis or an older Jimi. I bet that there a lot of people who, at one time, couldn't imagine an older Mercy, but here I am.

But Gram Parsons's death just broke my heart into pieces. Of all the deaths, that's the one that hurt the most. It still hurts, and it always will.

The first time I caught a glimpse of Gram was when Pamela and I attended the premiere of the Beatles' *Yellow Submarine* movie. I was a goner. He was so real, he was unreal. His ruby-red Nudie suit was sparkling in the dimmed theater, his rhinestone-cowboy belt slung around his lean, gunslinger hips, exaggerating his entrance into my life.

Pamela had always raved about Gram, but I was the only GTO who listened to her; the other girls weren't interested in what they foolishly dismissed as hillbilly music. I trusted Pamela, and she seemed to realize that Gram was way ahead of his time, crossing country music over to rock 'n' roll and vice versa and absolutely changing the direction of popular music. I for one welcomed a little Southern hospitality in my life as by this time I was bloody sick and tired of the 1960s British Invasion. Even though I was friends with Led Zeppelin and the Rolling Stones, I mostly resented the Brits; they pissed me off because I thought they wiped all the American music off the charts, ripped off the blues, and eradicated all our beloved teenage Italian idols. So when Pamela invited me to the outskirts of the San Fernando Valley to visit Gram and his fellow Flying Burrito Brothers Chris Hillman and Mike Clarke, I was up for the western adventure.

We drove to a modern cowboy ranch with wagon wheels paving the driveway, and Gram warmly welcomed us wearing one of his snazzy Nudie suits and holding a grocery bag full of grass. The first words I recall him speaking to me that day, as he leaned over a pile of vinyl and reached for a George Jones album, were, "This is George Jones, the king of broken hearts." And a tear literally dripped from his eye. It was the fuckin' corniest line, even if it sounded like poetry coming out of Gram's rosebud mouth. I almost burst out giggling. I looked at the cover photo of this square, country crooner on the George Jones LP and thought, "This Gram guy's a trip. Imagine crying over some hillbilly in a crewcut!" But then Gram put George's record on the turntable. I've been indebted to Gram ever since.

The other thing I remember Gram saying to me that day was "I want to shoot heroin." He hadn't done it yet.

I cocked my eyebrow and retorted, "Um, I don't think that's a very bright idea for you." But it pains me to say that we did shoot heroin together. I saw him go downhill really fast after that. When Gram started doing junk, he became a hopeless addict straight away. He became such a junkie that Keith Richards threw him out of France for being too loaded, saying, "I can't take it anymore, you're too stoned." Now, if *Keith Richards* is saying that, *that* is a *problem*. Within three years of me meeting him, Gram was dead.

At first Gram and I became friends because, frankly, we were fellow drug addicts. I rarely shot dope, but I did it with Gram. I would go visit him at the Chateau Marmont and spend the night, but it wasn't a sexual thing. I was attracted to him, but he didn't have a butt; he had a flat ass. But I loved him, and I loved his suits. Gram gave me an orange-and-white scarf that had belonged to Keith Richards, and he turned me onto the whole Nudie look; my main fashion goal in life soon became obtaining my very own "MERCY" belt in rhinestones, though I never did. Gram and I shared some wonderful times, staying up till dawn listening to Percy Sledge and holy roller tent revival albums that he brought back from New Orleans. We basically bonded over soul music and heroin. Sometimes we'd just watch TV, and I learned quickly that if I walked into Gram's place and *Hee Haw* was on, I had to be real quiet.

About three days before the Rolling Stones' infamous, disastrous Altamont Festival, where the Flying Burrito Brothers also performed, Pamela and I went to see Gram play a solo gig at the Corral Club in Topanga Canyon. Mick Jagger and Keith Richards were also there. The Stones adored Gram, and they derived a lot of inspiration from him; any country shtick they did basically came from Gram, and Keith will freely admit that. So, in walked the Stones. Mick already knew me but didn't know Pamela, and he called me over and said, "I'd like to know that girl, will you introduce me?"

Gram overheard this exchange and yelled out, "Hey, watch out, Pamela!" But I introduced them anyway. One thing led to another, and we all jumped in a limousine at the end of the night and went over to Peter Tork's house.

Mercy Fontenot *and* Lyndsey Parker

I remember an Otis Redding album was spinning, and Mick tore it off the turntable and put the Band on, because the Band were his new favorites: "This is the new thing we're listening to," he explained haughtily. Mick would do stuff like that. We were all sniffing cocaine, and it was spilling all over my vintage black velvet dress, which really freaked Mick out because he'd just gotten arrested in London and was very paranoid. To me, the coke powder scattered across the velvet sparkled like Nudie rhinestones; I thought it looked breathtaking.

The whole night had this feel of edginess, of agitation, even though we were having fun. I had my tarot cards with me, and for some dumb reason decided I was going to do a reading for the Stones. First I read Mick's cards, and I was scanning them nervously, thinking to myself, "*Okayyyy.* This is *not* good." The whole read-out was an utter tragedy. There was the Devil card, of course, which represents greed and obsession with power, and the final card was the Tower, which is a symbol for ambition constructed on faulty premises. I read Keith and Gram's cards next, and it was same alarming result. Just *no, no, no*—"no" was the one word going through my mind. All of the tarot cards looked horrible.

The Stones kept babbling about Altamont and how great it was going to be, how it was going to be the most fantastic festival of all time. And there I was with my cards, thinking, "Oh, my God, this is going to be just fucking hideous." But I decided not to tell them what I saw since I wasn't going to be able to change their minds about going through with it anyway. Mick in particular was not going to listen to anything I had to say because he clearly felt so above the law. Plus, Mick was a paranoid type as it was, even when he wasn't doing cocaine, and I didn't feel like upsetting him. So I just lied my ass off and told them everything would be awesome. But I knew there was trouble ahead. And everybody knows what happened at Altamont, when the violence broke out and the Hells Angels who'd been hired to be security guards stabbed that poor kid Meredith Hunter to death. Four people ultimately died that day—along with, many have said, the 1960s.

But three days after the party at Peter Tork's, against my better judgment, there I was, backstage at Altamont with Pamela and Ricky Prescott. And the first thing that I saw was Mick with a bloody mouth. He'd been slugged in the head by some fan the moment he stepped out of his helicopter. That certainly set the tone for the day. It all felt very dark and very gloomy, like a cloud was coming over everything, and I knew those tarot cards had been right. When the trouble started, there was lots of tugging and pulling. It looked like a mosh pit. Mick kept pleading with the crowd, "You've got to stop fighting. This is not right." I was already looking for an exit so I wouldn't get killed. Mick tried to prevent me from leaving, but I didn't feel any guilt about getting the hell out of there before disaster struck. I was despondent later when I heard about the stabbing, but mainly I was relieved that I didn't witness all that.

Pamela also went back to the hotel before things got rough. Michelle Phillips from the Mamas & the Papas was there too, looking for Gram, and later Mick showed up. Mick was losing his mind over what had happened at Altamont—pacing, freaking out, claiming he was never going to perform again. He asked Pamela to go back to his room with him, but because Michelle was there as well, and Pamela wrongly assumed that Mick wanted a threesome, she took off. Nothing went right for Mick that night.

The whole incident reminded me of another time I had a premonition, or some sort of sixth sense, when I was at the Rolling Stones' "Sympathy for the Devil" mixing session. Rodney Bingenheimer and I just happened to be hanging out, walking down Sunset, when Mick found out we were outside Sunset Sound studio and had an assistant invite us inside. When I heard Mick intoning,

"Who killed the Kennedys? / After all, it was you and me," I thought, "What is he doing? He is tempting fate. He's really messing with some Kenneth Anger-type shit here." It was satanic mastery. I don't believe Mick was seriously into the occult or devil worship, but I think he was toying with it because he thought it sounded mysterious and cool. Maybe he was just playing, but he was playing with fire, and it was all too heavy for me. So, when Altamont went down, I think it was all tied in.

I was always more impressed by Marianne Faithfull than by Mick. I thought she was so fucking fabulous. She was *everything* to me. What an incredible voice. I could relate to her song "Sister Morphine" so much because I had been arrested for morphine myself. I thought she was as beautiful as could be, but she was also sharp, witty, and genuinely nice. We became friends, and we'd trade stories and pills.

One time I was hitchhiking through Laurel Canyon and a limousine pulled up. Mick rolled down the window, just like the guy in that Grey Poupon commercial, and said, "Mercy, we can't find Frank Zappa's house. Can you take us?" Marianne was with him. So I hopped in the car and directed the driver to Frank's. Once inside, Marianne and I were trading pills by the house's bowling alley while Mick was in the kitchen chatting with Frank.

Frank always wanted to talk politics—that was his main thing, and when you talked politics with Frank, he always got you in a corner. But Mick was so high that night that he didn't have much of an opinion about anything. Frank eventually got so exasperated that he barked at Mick, "The next time you come up here, be a little bit more sober. And be more informed! I'm done with you." I was highly amused.

Many years later, in the nineties, I went to Marianne's book signing. I was still in love with her. I was all dressed up with my signature stacked belts and raccoon makeup, but I figured she wouldn't recognize me after all this time, so I just politely asked her to sign my copy. But Marianne flipped out. "Oh, my God, are you *kidding* me?!" she exclaimed. And then she shouted to everyone around us, "Do you *know* who this woman is? You won't believe who this woman is! This woman is *it*. If all you people knew who this woman was, you would be *amazed*." It was thrilling for me. I was so fucking freaked out. She signed one of my belts, too.

⚜

BACK TO GRAM PARSONS...GRAM really wanted to be on the GTOs album, but Frank said no. Gram pleaded, "Can't I even play tambourine?" But the answer was still no. I have no idea why. I thought Frank was insane. But Pamela and I eventually attended every Flying Burrito Brothers session there was, which cemented our lifelong friendship. Those sessions were certainly more enjoyable than the Stones' spooky "Sympathy for the Devil" one. We were always smoking pot, always loaded, but there were no heavy drugs allowed because the Burritos were very serious when they were working. Gram had some oxygen tanks in there to prevent headaches from being too high.

Pamela and I were at the Burritos' "Wild Horses" session at A&M Studios with Leon Russell on keyboards, and Leon was kind enough to lend me his coat when I was chilly. The entire experience was magical. When I first heard the song, I thought, "Oh, my God, this thing's a masterpiece." I was just enthralled by it. I was literally sitting there scribbling down the lyrics with a pen and paper because I'd never heard anything like it and I *needed* to remember what Gram was singing. I knew this music meant something. Just as Pamela had figured out before me, I knew Gram was going to explode, somewhere in time. I knew he held the key.

Mercy Fontenot *and* Lyndsey Parker

But I also knew that Gram would not be on this planet for very long. His delicate hands looked like Michelangelo had made them, and he seemed too sensitive for this world. I used to read his tarot cards at the Marmont, and they never looked very promising. He had a sense of doom all around him. Once again, I never warned Gram. Obviously, I was the worst tarot card reader in the world. But I could not even go there. I always tried to put a positive spin on the results and turn everything around.

The last time I saw Gram was when we passed each other in a courthouse. I had been busted for something, Lord knows what, and he had been busted while coming home from the Corral, though I forget what for. What I do remember is how he had bloated up so rapidly. He looked like he'd packed on about twenty-five pounds, and he had that same puffy face that Jim Morrison, Brian Jones, and Mark Bolan had in their later years. And then soon after that, Gram died. I could see it coming; he had nowhere to go but down. Still, it was the most devastating news I could've ever heard. It was like losing a member of the family.

Five years later, I was high on angel dust when Pamela and I went to see Robert Altman's brilliant country-music movie *Nashville*. Suddenly, back in a theater similar to the one where I'd first spotted Gram in all his Nudie-suited glory, I experienced these intense flashbacks and started bawling: "Oh, my God! Gram Parsons! Gram! *Grammmmmmmmm*!" Everyone was trying to calm me down and keep me quiet, but I was inconsolable. Gram was the kind of person that once you met him, you just never forgot him and never got over him.

Incidentally, I was in the famous gossip writer Rona Barrett's magazine in the eighties because my dear friend Cinnamon worked there, and I trashed Mick *so* badly. I called Mick a musical thief, the biggest charlatan I'd ever seen. I was still bitter because Gram was gone, and I thought Mick had done Gram wrong and never given credit where credit was due. I was also still mad about a time when I overheard Mick say he wished Brian Jones would die in a gutter, not long before Brian actually did die in a swimming pool. And then there'd been this other time when I told Mick I was working for Carla Thomas and he'd said to me, all snootily, "Oh, I *used* to like her"— which reminded me of that time when he yanked Otis Redding's LP off the record player. My resentment against Mick had been building for years, apparently. I doubt he even read Rona's column, or was upset if he did—but regardless, I don't regret a word.

6

Ice Cold Daydream

I ONCE HAD A dream that I was going to marry the great rock 'n' soul prodigy Shuggie Otis. Mind you, the dream didn't tell me that everything was going to be *wonderful*, or that it would last forever. It didn't tell me anything other than this was my fate and there was nothing I could do to change it. A Gypsy fortune-teller in New Orleans told me the same thing: "You can't run, you can't hide. You're going to marry this guy you're running away from."

In this dream I envisioned an exotic, striking, brown-skinned creature—more boy than man, with the trappings of feminine beauty—with a huge halo of Afro curls, sitting on a stool with his guitar. The next morning I jolted awake and thought, "I've just met my future husband." It was one of the many premonitions in my life that ultimately came true.

The day after my dream, Pamela and I were on our way to a Ringo Starr press conference, and I was telling her about my new "fiancé." She rolled her eyes, like she always did, as if to say, "Okay, Mercy, okay. Maybe ease up on the acid a bit?" But then I peered down at the car floor…and this soul angel from the dream, this vision, was staring back up at me. A music journalist who'd been assigned to review Al Kooper's *Kooper Session* album was in the car with us, and there was Shuggie on the cover of Kooper's album, next to my feet.

I looked at the LP cover and exclaimed, "Oh, my God, *that's* the guy I was talking about! Who is this person?"

And the journalist informed me, "His name is Shuggie Otis, and I'm reviewing his album. And you're *never* going to get to him because of his father, Johnny Otis." I was also told that Shuggie was fifteen years old—I was about nineteen at the time—but that didn't matter to me. I didn't think about that stuff. It was a different time. People even looked different back then; everyone dressed to look older. Anyway, we all ended up at the Ringo Starr event, then at a fancy hotel room after-party with Ahmet Ertegun, Graham Bond, and Michael Stoller, but the whole time I had Shuggie on the brain.

By the way, at the Ringo Starr event, Pamela got me in so much trouble because she made me ask Ringo if he'd ever heard of the GTOs; she actually forced me to raise my hand and ask him that. I believe Ringo said that he had. And then we got to Frank Zappa's house, and I never heard the end of it. Frank was so furious that I would embarrass the GTOs like that. Pamela set me up!

It took a while before I met Shuggie in real life, even though he'd actually played on the Zappa album *Peaches en Regalia*. But one day up in Topanga Canyon I mentioned my Shuggie dream to my friend Mike Kowalski, who played with the Beach Boys, and Mike said, "You know what? I know Shuggie Otis. I'm actually drumming for him on a session today at Columbia Records. Do you want to go?" Of *course* I wanted to go. And that is how I met Shuggie Otis.

People ask me if I felt a spark right away, if sparks flew. Well, I felt a spark before I ever met Shuggie. The sparks had already flown, at least for me. I didn't get the sense that Shuggie was physically attracted to me. *I* wouldn't be attracted to me, to be honest. I was cute, I guess, but I was heavyset and weird-looking. Shuggie did write me a letter after we were together that said, "Nobody knows how beautiful that you are, but I do." I didn't know what the hell that meant. It was a sort of backhanded compliment.

Still, that afternoon I could tell that Shuggie was *intrigued* by me. That pessimistic music journalist had been correct, though, when he'd warned me that Johnny Otis would try to stand in my way. Johnny was there in the studio, eyeing me up and down with this steely expression as if to say, "No way, José." I couldn't blame him. I was some white freak, and Johnny had lofty ambitions for his phenomenally talented son. So, okay, this wasn't going to be the right moment to make my move. But I was going to get to Shuggie eventually. He was on my list, after all.

Johnny scared the fuck out of me at first. I didn't know his background, didn't realize he was bona fide rock 'n' roll royalty. I knew he'd had a hit record, "Willie and the Hand Jive," but I had no idea how important he truly was. This was a man who'd discovered or worked with Jackie Wilson, Little Willie John, Etta James, and Esther Phillips (whose junkie song "Home Is Where the Hatred Is" could be the theme music of my life), and he hosted his own radio and TV shows in the fifties. Johnny was a little prejudiced, and very cynical about the music business—he had seen it all and was not easily impressed—and it was hard for him to emerge from his old ways. He was only about fifty-five, but at the time I thought that was positively ancient.

Johnny had grown up in a predominantly Black neighborhood and had always passed for Black—which was good for his early career, because back in those days a white man could not be caught on a tour bus with "colored" musicians. Someone probably would have beat the hell out of him, or even hanged the rest of his band. On tour, Johnny would actually be turned away from both white and

Black hotels. He'd had crosses burned on his lawn. So he was wary of white people. Once he said in front of me, "Shuggie could've had any girl in the world. He could've had any woman. I was hoping for someone who was Black."

But Johnny had immense esteem for talented white musicians, and he played a large part in helping eradicate the whole concept of "white music" versus "Black music" that had existed in my early radio-listening days. One time in *Rolling Stone* I saw a photograph from the 1950s of Johnny with the very white Everly Brothers, which surprised me. "Why are you with the Everly Brothers here?" I asked Johnny.

And he said, "Because the Everly Brothers could *sing*."

Johnny and I ultimately connected over music. We used to talk about the Everlys, Billy Joe Royal, the blues. One time, he called me on the phone and started asking me all these R&B trivia questions. I answered them easily and he marveled, "Oh, my God, you sure know a lot!" He was testing me. He eventually came to respect me, and I always kind of had a crush on Johnny, too. I know saying that will get me in trouble! It was more like I was in awe of him.

Shuggie, who was half Black, could be pretty prejudiced too. He would complain all the time about "white motherfuckers," though he obviously didn't have a problem with dating white girls. Shuggie and I became friends at first. I was at his house a lot, always putting myself in his path. Or actually, he put me in *his* path—he'd come pick me up, and I would take him out to dress him up in antique velvets and satins, sort of acting as his stylist. Drugs were at the center of his life and mine, besides his music. And his music was basically fueled by drugs at that time. Drugs were definitely something we bonded over. We partied all the time.

Somewhere along the line, it crossed into romance. It was probably because of my friendship with Jimi Hendrix, whom Shuggie worshipped. One night I was at Jimi's Forum concert with Chuck

Wein, and I glanced up and spotted Shuggie's billowing Afro hairdo way up in the nosebleed seats—because *that's* how big his Afro was. Shuggie noticed I was sitting pretty in the third row, and that clearly impressed him. And then I went off to Hawaii to shoot Jimi's movie *Rainbow Bridge*, and that sealed the deal. I confess, my main motivation for being in *Rainbow Bridge* at all was Shuggie. I wanted to grab his attention. I thought, "Oh, my God, Shuggie will just flip out!" And he did.

I've always said three people discovered my existence: Baron Wolman, Frank Zappa, and Chuck Wein. I met Chuck on the night of the drug bust that led to the downfall of the GTOs, so it was a classic case of one door closing and another opening. Chuck ended up doing a movie called *Arizona Slim* with Pamela later, which is how Pamela met Michael Des Barres, so Chuck was instrumental in making two of the GTOs' marriages happen, in a way. For *Rainbow Bridge*, he said, "Mercy, I want you in this." And he put me on a plane to Hawaii.

We were on the island of Maui shooting *Rainbow Bridge* for a few weeks. I'm not sure how long I was there, exactly. It was too long, I'll tell you that. I hated it. It was too much like being in a flat postcard; seriously, Hawaii was very beautiful, but very boring. I was staying in a girls' school dormitory; there was nothing to do except look at pretty scenery. And the only drug I could score was Maui Wowie marijuana.

Jimi was unusually quiet, not very conversational, during the making of *Rainbow Bridge*. I didn't spend much time with him on the set. He hung out with Melinda Merryweather, the art director, and that was about it. He basically stayed to himself, and he had to get totally stoned to do his scenes. I think the crew got him high on angel dust, or maybe some psychedelic. My conspiracy theory is that he had trouble doing one scene because it foretold his death, a scene in which he talks about being with Cleopatra and choking on a grape. There's been speculation for years that Jimi was wine-boarded to death by mafia hitmen. So, if you believe that, then he really *did* choke on a grape.

Another time on the set when I got the premonition that Jimi wasn't long for this world was when I saw him disappear. I saw him do that teleportation, beam-me-up-Scotty thing. As he was coming over the bridge toward me, he kind of *Star Trekked* out. He became a hologram right in front of my eyes. I used to see visions like that all the time, and when I did, I knew the person would soon leave this planet. Jimi died about two months after *Rainbow Bridge* wrapped.

I spent most of my Hawaii downtime with one of the film's producers, Barry De Prendergast, and Clara Shuff, the *Enquirer's* psychic. I was "engaged" to Barry for a while, even though he was totally gay. I was engaged all the time, but my fiancés were always gay. Barry and I never had an affair, but he loved me for some reason, and I loved him right back. Clara was something else. She did a reading for me, and for Jimi too, but I could never understand that woman. Still, it was exciting to have her there. When we filmed the one scene on the beach, she had to be turned around because she could not look at the reflections in the water—she was too clairvoyant to deal with those frequencies. Sometimes on the bus with the crew, I'd sit back and observe Dr. Emanuel Bronner and Clara gabbing away in their native tongue, German.

Shooting the Dr. Bronner lecture scene was my favorite part of the *Rainbow Bridge* experience. Dr. Bronner was a German Jew, a genius, and allegedly the nephew of Albert Einstein. I mean, we all know his Magic Soap. His soap labels have so much information printed on them, it's like reading a book about Magic Soap. He was brimming with big ideas. He told us all that fluoride hardened our teeth and arteries and it was going to kill us and should be labeled as poison. He talked about Halley's Comet, about Moses, and how we are all beasts and not yet human. Even an atheist would appreciate this stuff. All this information was astounding, and I soaked it all in like an especially porous sponge. You can see in the scenes where they cut to me, how intently I'm listening. I have like five pairs of eyelashes on, and I'm staring straight through them.

I had one big scene. I looked heavy in it, unfortunately. I did a Tarzan dance on the rocks by a waterfall with a teeny tyke named Tiff—a cute little dude who resembled a junior Bernardo. Chuck told me, "Just go to work, Mercy," and I did it in one take. I let out a crazy Tarzan jungle cry and ripped my dress in two pieces—that was all improv. In the final, edited version, everything is slowed down to look like a 1920s silent movie.

Jimi's concert itself was really remarkable. There was a fantastic closeup of me strolling to the park for the concert, dramatically trailing a scarlet veil. Sadly, there's a missing scene of me and these groupie girls, the Gemini twins, dancing onstage. I ran into somebody years later who informed me, "You know, I have that footage. You can come to my house and see it, but I can't let it out. Nobody's supposed to know I have it." I never did see it.

When I first saw *Rainbow Bridge*, I wore a rainbow wig to the premiere and was buzzing with excitement, but I didn't understand the movie at all. I went, "Oh, my God, what a piece of crap. How dumb is this?" But it didn't really matter because the main reason I had done the film was to get in with Shuggie, and I further ingratiated myself by taking him as my date to the premiere. From that point on, my dream started to become reality.

One night Johnny, Carla Thomas, Shuggie, and I went on a double date of sorts—it was a platonic thing between Johnny and Carla, but I obviously wanted it to be more than platonic between me and Johnny's son. Johnny had a truck and Shuggie and I were squeezed together in the back, and we started making out. That's when that started.

Sometimes on our private dates, in the car I would get all goopy and either give Shuggie head or jack him off while he was driving. I suppose that was dangerous, but those were hardly my most dangerous experiences riding in cars. The first time Shuggie and I ever actually had sex was at his parents' house. His brother was there in the bedroom, in the other bed. Shuggie just took me home and we did the deed, and it was really vanilla but really nice. If I am being honest, Shuggie was not amazing in the sack. He was young, four years younger than me, and he had a lot to learn. Honestly, so did I. It was difficult for me to be in an intimate relationship with someone I so desperately idolized. It didn't make for a very equal dynamic. The whole time I'd be inwardly thinking, "Oh, my God!" and practically pinching myself; Shuggie almost didn't seem real to me, and that made it impossible to even be in the moment. He'd touch me and I would just fall to pieces. But it meant so much to me every time I was with him.

All this time, other women were chasing Shuggie, like all the Hendrix groupies, and this chick Sunshine that he disappeared with for two days, and the gorgeous muse Fayne Pridgon. I knew there was nothing I could do to stop this. But I wasn't jealous. Sunshine even called me and admitted, "I know Shuggie loves you and you really love him." And Fayne in particular was the woman who'd inspired "Foxey Lady" and had introduced Sam Cooke to Jimi Hendrix, and was a great blues singer in her own right and best friends with Etta James, so I honestly thought it was just marvelous that she was hanging around. In the beginning, Shuggie and I were both having outside affairs because we were not together as an official couple.

There was really only one woman that made me jealous, and that was Lillian Wilson, known to most as "Teri," the daughter of famous bandleader Gerald Wilson and the woman who would one day become Shuggie's second wife.

Teri was there all along, always in the background. Really, she was there first. Shuggie and Teri had known each other all their lives and were supposedly like brother and sister, but I knew she was in love with him. She had a big crush on him from high school, and her sister was going with Nicky, Shuggie's younger brother, so she was always over at the Otis house. It's odd that I was so jealous of the person that, deep down, I knew Shuggie was destined to be with. Something had sparked between them way early on, and I merely came in and put the temporary brakes on what was going to happen sooner or later. I do feel like Teri was Shuggie's destiny. When they were together, it was clear they were soulmates. Eventually it got to the point where I couldn't fight that.

Teri and I were friends at first. She kind of idolized me, like she thought I was very cool, and I kind of idolized her. But soon the jealousy set in. One time Shuggie and I went to a Johnny "Guitar" Watson club gig and he brought Teri. She was the third wheel— or *I* was really the third wheel, but I didn't realize that until later. Afterward, we got in the car and Shuggie said, "Mercy, I'm going to drop you off first, and then I'll drop Teri off." He clearly wanted to be alone with Teri. I was so upset that I jumped out of the car in the middle of the night somewhere. I didn't even know where I was. I was *that* kind of crazy then. Looking back with regret, I think I really should have gone after Johnny "Guitar" Watson that night because that man was *fine*.

Shuggie could get ragingly, irrationally jealous as well, even though he had absolutely no right to be. He was an explosive guy, totally wild, a typical unstable genius. At first I was flattered by it and thought his unhealthy jealousy was a sign that he really cared. One time I went up to San Francisco to emcee the Cockettes' show with Sylvester and the Pointer Sisters, and when I came back, Shuggie commanded, "Don't you *ever* go someplace without telling me again!"

At the time, I thought it was cool. I thought, "Okay, there must be something going on here. He must dig me."

Later on, it was not cool. Shuggie actually shredded my diaries that Frank Zappa was going to have published. I heard these ripping noises coming from the bedroom, so I flung open the door and there were my journal pages, strewn all over. I don't have my diaries anymore because of Shuggie; ironically, most of my diary entries were all about him! He also destroyed all the albums of any man that he knew or suspected I had slept with—he even wrecked albums in his dad's record collection. One time he almost strangled me. I don't know what our argument was about, but his father came in and slapped him, and got him off me. Johnny had never hit Shuggie before, and I appreciated him sticking up for me. I wish I still had those diaries, though. They sure would have made writing this book much easier.

One time I actually tried to make Shuggie jealous, but I epically failed.

Chuck Berry was playing a concert with Johnny Otis at Disneyland, and I went with Shuggie and the Otis family to see the show. Before we set off, I gulped down a handful of pharmaceutical pills—Valiums, whatever I could find. I was self-medicating because Teri was on the bus too, and I was stressed by her presence. She was always a threat. I was so out of it by the time we arrived in Anaheim that as soon as we all got off the bus, I collapsed in the bushes. Supposedly this got Johnny Otis kicked out of Disneyland forever, I'm not really sure. That's what Johnny told me. If that's true, I am sorry.

When I crawled out of the foliage, I realized Shuggie had vanished somewhere with Teri, without helping me up or even checking to see if I was okay. "Fuck this," I thought. Disneyland hardly felt like the happiest place on earth at that moment. So there I was, backstage by myself, loaded out of my mind on this dark and misty night, when this old Cadillac came creeping up. And out of the car emerged the one and only Chuck Berry. I had always idolized him, ever since the first time I saw him on *Ed Sullivan*. I still think he was brilliant, like the Bob Dylan of early rock 'n' roll—and really the first groupie song was "Sweet Little 16" by Chuck Berry, if you think about it. I thought he was a little bit of an old man by then, but he still was gorgeous. He had a bit of Native American in him, with high, sculpted cheekbones. So, without even thinking, I blurted out, "I've been waiting to meet you all my life! This is what I've been waiting for!"

Without missing a beat, Chuck said, "Let's go." And we climbed into his private trailer.

I most likely had sex with Chuck that night, but I can't be sure because I was so out of my mind on pills that it's all a blur. Nowadays, there is a lot of talk about consent, and, yes, many would argue that if I was too loaded to remember this sexual encounter, then it was assault or rape. But I've been raped plenty of times, so I know what rape feels like—and I *don't* consider this Chuck encounter a crime. I was no victim here. I would've done it anyway, stone-cold sober. Well, maybe not the bucket thing—I wouldn't do *that* in my right mind. But all the other stuff, I would have happily consented to, no matter what.

So…about that bucket. Chuck Berry was known for certain bathroom fetishes and peeping-Tom behavior, for which he got in big, big trouble later. After we finished doing whatever we did in his trailer, he informed me, "I'm going to take a photo of you because I always take pictures of the women I have sex with." So obviously we must have had sex, even if I don't remember it. Anyway, I let him take a naked Polaroid. I don't know where that photograph is now. I'd actually like to see it. Then he said, "Would you do me another favor? I'm going to hand you a bucket. I would like you to go to the bathroom and take a shit while I watch." At the time, I thought Chuck's request was odd, but I was probably too fucking high to process it. So what the hell—I did as I was asked. I gave him his sexy stool sample. I don't even want to know what he did with the bucket afterward. At least there's no Polaroid of me doing that, thank God.

Suddenly, there was a knock at the trailer door: "Mr. Berry, you're on now!"

Chuck asked me, "Hey, could you do me a favor and carry my guitar for me?" Of course I said yes. I thought, "Awesome, I get to go home with Chuck Berry, the greatest cat ever that started rock 'n' roll!" And as I was lugging Chuck's guitar to the stage, I also stupidly thought, "Oh, wow, Shuggie's totally going to see this. Boy, will he be jealous!" But there was nobody backstage to see it. The backstage area was a ghost town. Damn it! That was super annoying. And then Chuck's girlfriend turned up, so I would not be going home with Chuck after all. But I guess Chuck was another notable notch on my belt—my many layered belts.

I ended up stumbling back onto the bus after the gig and going home with Shuggie and Teri. Later that night, I told Shuggie that I had screwed Chuck Berry, just to mess with Shuggie's head. Shuggie was pissed, but he had no reason to be. We weren't an exclusive couple yet, and besides, he had disappeared with Teri, which had pissed *me* off. All day, I had felt like Shuggie's number two...and then I actually went "number two" for Chuck.

Shuggie was very hard to get close to. Shuggie was interested in Shuggie, basically. Shuggie was his own number one. As I struggled to get closer to him and insert myself between him and Teri, I isolated myself from everybody else. My jealousy was starting to get the better of me, and I would never bring over someone like Connie Gripp to the Otis house. I didn't even want Pamela around Shuggie; I knew

Pamela was a true-blue friend and would never, ever go after him, but my mindset was all warped.

I decided I had to get away, far away. Shuggie was overshadowing everything, dominating my life, and I didn't like it one bit. He was all I thought about, and I started to obsess over the possibility that maybe I wouldn't or couldn't ever land him. Even though I'd had a dream about marrying him, there was always this duality, a fear of rejection, a fear that the dream would not come true. It was time to go pursue another dream for a while.

7

I Can't Get Next to You

MOST OF THE LA girls wanted to go to London to hang with the Beatles and shop on Kings Road at Granny Takes a Trip. I wanted to take a trip to Memphis instead. My parole officer was a Black sympathizer, a white woman totally into Black culture like me—I was reading *Soul on Ice*, the Eldridge Cleaver/Black Panther book, and I was really dedicated to it, and she was too—and we shared a bond. So I figured she'd understand why I needed to go chase the Stax sound.

All my life, I've sought out and gravitated toward the energy centers—certain places that I knew would be important to musical history. Haight-Ashbury, the Blue Unicorn, and the Fillmore harnessed that energy. Zappa's Log Cabin had it. Later in my life, I'd find it at punk clubs like the Masque and Cathay de Grande. And I already knew that Stax Records in Memphis had it, even before I got there. That's why I had to go there, to get close to it. I wanted to know absolutely everything about the Stax sound—how it was made, who was making it.

Frankly, I also wanted to get to know the Bar-Kays, a far-out young soul group that I crushed on madly. The Bar-Kays were dressing like

Rick James before Rick James, they were punk before punk—leather spacesuits, metal spikes, Afro wigs—and I was utterly obsessed. I was in awe of the Bar-Kays when I first laid eyes on them. So I decided, "I'm going to go to Memphis and find them." Plus, Memphis was 2,000 miles away...which meant Shuggie couldn't reach me there. Shuggie was all I thought about—besides the Bar-Kays, that is—and this fixation was driving me bonkers. So, it was Memphis or bust.

Somehow I convinced my gal pal Marquise, who was Marlowe B. West's cousin, to join me on my pilgrimage, and we hitchhiked to our destination. And then, there we were, two lily-white California girls in the Stax Records parking lot, in a very Black neighborhood: Marquise the flamed-haired, porcelain-skinned beauty queen, and me the panda-eyed Gypsy witch. I had no grand master plan. I couldn't explain to Marquise what was supposed to happen next. But then out sashayed the beautiful Bar-Kays through Stax's doors.

The Bar-Kays only waved casually at us...before they piled into cars with their protective moms. Most of them were around sixteen years old, so our dreams of going home with any of them were quickly shattered. But before I had a moment to wonder if this journey had been a colossal waste of time, following close behind the Bar-Kays was another soul combo—a little older and a lot more conservative, but a lot friendlier.

I didn't realize at first that these were the Hodges brothers— Teenie, Leroy, and Charles, the premier rhythm section of the day. An adorable one approached us, introduced himself as Teenie, and invited us to a different studio, explaining that they had just recorded with Sir Mack Rice and were headed to another session with some up-and-coming bright new soul star. We were stranded anyway, and these cats had real appeal, so it made sense to tag along. And thus, we were rescued by Teenie Hodges. Teenie wasn't a flashy cat, but he was charming—and familiar, as if from a past lifetime.

He would become our Memphis tour guide. Somehow, I really trusted him, and I knew he wasn't going to do anything nutty. My inner voice told me to follow him.

And so, off we went to our first stop, literally across the tracks, to Royal Studios, the humble recording headquarters for Hi Records and the Hi Rhythm Section. This was a small eight-track studio with clientele like Ike & Tina booked, not that well-known yet. But it was most definitely another energy center. I had another one of my famous and almost-always-correct premonitions that what was emanating from Royal Studios that day was going to change the world.

It was here that I was exposed to the first sacred instrumental tracks for the Hodges' mysterious new vocalist. These guys simply picked up their instruments and instantly orchestrated an avalanche of soul-shattering sonic booms—no gimmicks, no distortion, just a gumbo of R&B, country and western, and funk, a groove that made me move. They laid down one funky cut after another, after another, after another, after another, after another. Boom, boom, boom, boom, boom. It was so tight that all it took was one take. Willie Mitchell, the magnificent maestro himself, mixed the sound. Teenie was freaking me out on guitar. He's still my favorite guitarist to this day because he did rhythm leads like nobody else.

I kept thinking to myself, "Where am I? This is *insane!*" I'd been to other sessions, sure, but they weren't like this. This band was so tight. It was unbelievable. I totally was in awe. I knew something was going on. This sound was royal, just like the studio's name, and these were the princes. But I had yet to meet the king.

After this session, our young minds still reeling from what we had just witnessed, Marquise and I squeezed back in the car with the Hodges princes, who told us, "We want to introduce you to our new lead singer." We drove across town to a nondescript, middle-class, suburban neighborhood, entered through an unfurnished house full of unpacked boxes, and were greeted in a soft, unassuming voice by this slim, conservative-looking Black cat in a trench coat, Al Green. Al was cute but very square, sort of like an African American Frank Sinatra. I was not impressed. In fact, Al was so straight-looking that he actually weirded me out. I was used to freaky Black dudes like Shuggie Otis, Jimi Hendrix, and the space-alien Bar-Kays. Al was way too smooth for me.

We all got in the car to cruise the record shops so Al could purchase his new hit single blasting every twenty minutes on the Memphis AM radio station. Al was riding the crest of local fame with "I Can't Get Next to You," but I'd never heard the song on Los Angeles radio before. It sounded pretty good, but I still didn't quite get it. Al socialized with shop owners and fans, checked his sales, dropped off a stack of autographed photos, and then we went to the outskirts of town to cop some weed. It was during this errand run that Al asked me if I wanted to stay the night with him, and I flat-out turned him down. I would soon come to regret this decision.

To be honest, I didn't start to have an attraction to Al until I heard him sing like a nightingale. That's when I fell, hard. After we headed back to Royal to cut his vocals that day, when he opened his mouth to sing, my mouth opened too—as in, my jaw *dropped*. I was surprised that came out of his mouth. But I would be surprised if that came out of *anybody's* mouth, okay? I'd never heard any voice that magnificent except for Otis Redding's, but this was a different vibe from Otis. I thought, "Oh, my God, now I don't care how straight Al looks. This guy is going to be the biggest thing to hit the charts." This was to be one of the most important sessions in music history, producing "I'm Still in Love With You." I fell under Al's spell, but just as the song "I Can't Get Next to You" said, I couldn't get next to him at that time. I'd missed my chance. Later that week I went to the phone booth and called

Al, hoping to take him up on his offer—but some chick answered the phone, so that killed that.

That evening, we all got loaded and hit up the famous nightspot Hernando's Hideaway, where the house band was led by the amazing Ronnie Milsap; the club was full, and everyone there seemed to be a historian of rock: Steve Cropper, Booker T., Donald "Duck" Dunn. This joint, where the Blacks and whites could freely mix and mingle on the outskirts of town, would become my regular hangout during my stay in Memphis. Another night, Marquise and I went there with the Bar-Kays and some people from Stax, and Maceo Parker put on an incredible show for hours and hours. And at the end of it he came walking up to me and said, "Was I good? Did I do a good job?"

I looked at him and gasped, "Are you *kidding* me? Were you 'good'? Are you really kidding me?"

After Milsap's set, Steve Holt, the drummer, invited me and Marquise over and off we went to Steve's mother's old two-story house; she occupied the first floor, and Steve and a pimp named Pretty Jimmy Red lived in the upstairs unit. Teenie stealthily dropped us off first and took Al home because in those days it was not acceptable for white girls to be in a car with Black guys in certain sections of Memphis. The police could get brutal sometimes.

Steve brought out the angel dust, also known as elephant tranquilizer, and we proceeded to puff and party. In Memphis, angel dust was the most popular drug around, and it was fabulous. It was like being in *Alice in Wonderland*. You took one hit and you were high all day. Angel dust always lived up to its name for me, because when I smoked it the dead contacted me—and this was occurring again. I stared at a framed photograph on Steve's desk of him with a group of young Black musicians, and it read, "The Bar-Kays." Steve told me that this was his group originally, but that supposed threats on Otis

Redding's life had scared him into quitting. Otis had died in a plane crash that also killed most of the original Bar-Kays. There are many people—including, frankly, myself—who entertained conspiracy theories that the crash was no "accident."

The Bar-Kays that I had followed out to Memphis were actually the second generation of the rebooted group, led by trumpeter Ben Cauley, the only survivor of the plane crash, and bassist James Alexander, who hadn't been on the plane because there wasn't enough room for an eighth passenger that doomed night. Ben and I eventually became good friends, and the poor guy talked about the crash all the time. It was awful, the most terrible thing; it ruined his life to see his friends reaching for him, crying out for help, and he couldn't do anything to help them. He saw them go down in front of him, and he never, ever got over it.

I wouldn't say I felt like an outsider in Memphis. Maybe I *should* have felt unsafe, but it was other people that felt unsafe because of us, fearing for their own safety when hanging with us. I was naive to what was really happening, and I wasn't aware of the situation I was in because Hollywood was its own liberal bubble. Inside the Memphis studios or the nightclubs it was racially mixed and everything was cool, but the general climate of civilian Memphis was an entirely different situation. Teenie would warn me and Marquise, "We have to watch what we're doing here. If anybody sees us in this area, they'll stop us and kill us." When we drove around town with the Hodges guys, he'd order us to duck down before someone saw two young white women riding in a car with Black men.

Teenie later put me and Marquise up in the Lorraine Motel, where Martin Luther King Jr. had been assassinated only a year before. I didn't realize that or didn't make the connection politically; I was really kind of dumb. I didn't understand that the climate in town was very heavy. But I always figured no one was going to bother us because the Hodges brothers were stars in Memphis, and they were our protectors. I listened to Teenie and always stuck to the safe musical havens that he escorted us to.

One night Teenie took me and Marquise to see Ike and Tina Turner at the Paradise Bowling Alley. We were the only two white girls in there, but nobody thought anything of it because we were with Teenie. After the show, Ike made a beeline straight to us—or more specifically to Marquise, who was a beautiful, beautiful girl. Ike commanded, "Come on, you two. Come backstage with me."

And so we did, and then we followed Ike to the motel after-party. There, he led us to the bathroom, where a whole mound of cocaine awaited us. I was sniffing the hell out of it. But Ike's cousin, a lesbian, kept knocking on the bathroom door, calling out to me, "Can you get on the bed with me, so that we can entertain Ike?" Ike already had a girl-on-girl scene going on in the next room for his party guests' amusement, two lesbians on the bed going at it, and I guess he wanted me to join in on that action. I told his cousin that I couldn't because I was with my "wife"—pretending Marquise and I were a couple and we were faithful—and that's how I got rid of this crazy chick. Finally she got the message and found another willing partner, and they went to town on the bed where everybody could see it. I paid them absolutely no mind. Ike didn't really watch either—I really think he was just trying to entertain his friends.

Ike kept talking about how he used to hate white people because they murdered his father, or so he claimed—some white people allegedly buried his father's remains underneath the house, and the rotting odor would waft up through the floorboards, and he could smell it. The stench forever haunted him. But then he changed his mind about white people after his tour bus broke down on the side of the road one day and nobody would help him but white people, which made him realize that some white people were good and kind. This was his story. Okay, then. I just kept doing the coke.

I idolized Ike, and just being around him—along with his blow—was enough to satisfy me. But Marquise later disappeared with Ike for the whole night, and I was left in the room alone with all these weird party people. I found out later that nothing happened between Ike and Marquise, that they just talked. We had a photo taken with Ike that night, but Marquise's jealous husband found it years later and tore it up.

I deeply wanted to stay in Memphis forever. It felt like my true spiritual home. But I was still on probation from the GTOs drug bust, and my kindly officer wrote me a letter warning me that I had to get home or I'd be arrested. Besides, it was probably my fate that I'd be pulled back to Los Angeles eventually. Even in Memphis, I could not escape from Shuggie Otis. The night that I smoked angel dust with Steve Holt, we were watching television, and I looked at the TV set... and there was Shuggie, live from the Ash Grove, on *The Johnny Otis Show*. I thought, "My God, where can I go? Is there *anywhere* I can go to get away from this man?"

So, I made it back to Hollywood and quickly fell back in with Shuggie. But I hadn't stopped plotting how to get my second chance with the one that got away, Al Green. In the meantime, I landed my dream job as the assistant to Sandy Newman, manager for the Bar-Kays, Albert King, Rufus Thomas, and my favorite female singer, Carla Thomas. Back in LA I had become friends with Carla, and I invited her to *The Johnny Otis Show* because I was still chasing Shuggie. Johnny had told me, grudgingly, "Well, if you bring Carla, then you can come." So we went, and Carla brought Sandy with her.

For some reason, at the end of the day, Sandy asked if I wanted to work for her. Of course I said, "Yes. Yes, I would like that. I would like that very much."

Working for Sandy was the greatest job in the world. I was getting paid to club-hop with the Bar-Kays, spend quality time with Carla, and hang on the set of *Soul Train*. I was honored to be on the *Soul Train* set about six or seven times, though I never danced on the show. They wouldn't let me; white people could not dance on that show at that time. I'm not saying that was an *official* rule, but that was my impression, so I didn't press it. It didn't bother me much because I was all for the Black Power movement. "Let them have this," I thought. Maybe my feelings were a little hurt that I couldn't participate, but what right did I have to be dancing on *Soul Train* anyway? I couldn't move and groove like those cool kids did.

During my time working for Sandy, I also had the huge privilege of attending the Wattstax festival. To me, Wattstax was the greatest musical event since Monterey Pop. I thought of it as actually the Black Monterey Pop, or the Black Woodstock. That's where the best music of the era was really coming from. What an amazing show. They really politically socked it to 'em that day, taking over the Los Angeles Coliseum at a time when the civil rights movement was basically still going on. It was a huge coliseum full of Black people that had Black power, and the vibe was excellent. These people had found their home. The music was changing everything, getting deeper into the psychological aspects of being Black, and uplifting the masses at the same time. The Reverend Jesse Jackson was there, flashing the peace sign. Richard Pryor was there. This was one of those moments, like Monterey Pop, where I knew it was important and historic at the time, not in hindsight.

There weren't many white people at Wattstax, other than me and Connie Gripp, but at first I felt accepted by the crowd, and nobody really bothered us. I actually *loved* that there were no white people there. But eventually I did not feel very welcome. The vibe became kind of overwhelming. It's not that anybody started anything with us, it's just that I didn't want anything *to* start. When Rufus Thomas came on, there was a lot of fence-jumping, so I split during that, just because I thought, "What the hell's going to happen? Are the police going to come in?" That might have happened, but thankfully it didn't.

Sadly, I only worked for Sandy for about a year. I had to quit after Shuggie and I got serious—not so much because Shuggie didn't want me to work, but because he certainly did not want me to work around the Bar-Kays. I couldn't blame him. No man should let his old lady spend a lot of time around the Bar-Kays. I'd be jealous of the Bar-Kays if I were a guy. I actually had a bit of a tryst with one of the Bar-Kays. I won't divulge which one, and I cannot explain it—I ended up in a hotel room with him, and something happened in bed. I don't know exactly what it was, but he only used his feet; that's all I will say. But that was a one-time thing. To be honest, I would have liked to have been with *any* of the Bar-Kays, because I thought they were all adorable. That was atypical of me; I usually only crushed on one member of a group. But anyway, I didn't cross that line again. Shuggie saw to it that I didn't.

Before I fully committed to Shuggie, however, I still had some unfinished business to take care of.

Soon after I returned to LA, Al Green became as big a pop star as a man could get, a huge idol. He was totally at the top, charting everywhere, breaking musical barriers. So I wrote him a letter—a real flowery, X-rated, super-sexual letter, telling him all the things I yearned to do with him, if I could finally spend the night with him like I should have back in Memphis. I figured my letter would likely just end up on a pile of unopened fan mail, but it was worth a try. I don't remember exactly what the letter said, but when I want to write, I really *write*. I'm effective. Whatever I wrote, it worked. Al called me up at the Wilton Hilton, where I was living at the time, and gasped in disbelief, "Did you *really* write that?" I told him yes—every single word came from my dirty little mind. And he said, "Well, when I get out to LA, I'm coming to see you."

Al was a man of his word, and he rang me up when he was in California. The first time he called me was from Disneyland, and I missed him. The second time, I was thankfully at home, and Al was playing the Forum. I walked through the Wilton Hilton door with Shuggie—it was the night Sugarcane Harris played the Whisky—and my landlady Donna Bates yelled out, "Al's on the phone!" Shuggie had been hanging with the famous groupie Fayne Pridgon lately and wasn't even trying to hide that affair from me —Shuggie and I were not an exclusive couple yet, and he could go his way, I could go mine—so I shrugged and said, right in front of Shuggie, "Okay, let me talk to Al."

Al said, "Meet me at the Continental Hyatt House. Did you really mean what you said in the letter? Come over right now." I said sure and took off.

I put on my favorite beautiful white vintage Moroccan robe, which had a 1940s Katharine Hepburn effect, and headed over. When Al opened the door, he blurted, "Oh, my God, you look fantastic. You've lost some weight. *Wow*." We smoked some pot and Al put on his own records, which I thought was a weird choice for mood music, and we had straight sex. It didn't get into anything beyond normal sexual intercourse, nothing like the stuff I said in my letter—just your basic positions. That was as far as it went. It was no big thing. Compared to his sexy, swaggering persona, it was a letdown. Maybe he was just tired after playing the Forum, but I thought, "Is that all there really is to the guy who is the biggest sex god on the planet, supposedly Mr. Sex himself?" But I was in love with somebody else, so perhaps that killed the emotion I might have been able to feel otherwise. My heart was still with Shuggie at this point, so I wasn't going to try to fuel anything to go further.

I was just happy to have had that intimate time with Al, that one night, that one memory.

Sex has never been a big deal for me. I slept with Al right after he'd played to thousands of people at the Forum, when he was at the top of his game, and *that* was the reason to do it. Going to bed with Al Green was just an accomplishment, just a notch on my belt. I did like Al, and I could have even loved him, but I was in love with Shuggie.

That was the last time I saw Al. I spent the night, and as I was leaving the Hyatt the next day, he reached into a briefcase full of the money he got paid the night before and handed me five dollars—out of thousands and thousands of dollars—and told me to take a taxicab home. As I opened the hotel room door, two women fell at my feet. They worked for Al, and I understand that later on they ended up blackmailing him.

Amusingly, one time Johnny Otis was talking to me about Al Green; he had no idea I'd slept with Al, of course. Johnny told me he thought Al Green was gay, and I said, "Gee, that's funny, because he sure wasn't when I was with him!"

I don't tend to consider anyone, including Al, "the one that got away." But looking back, I would say that Teenie Hodges fits that bill. After Shuggie, Teenie was the other great love of my life. Emotionally—*emotionally*, not sexually—Teenie captured my heart because of the way he took care of me and Marquise. Teenie always made sure that we were safe and was totally on guard for us, and I really loved him for it. I never forgot him. When I left Memphis, he stayed in my mind all the time. I was always talking about him. Recently I watched an old episode of *Art Fein's Poker Party* that I was on, from around 1987, and I'm sitting there, babbling on and on about Teenie Hodges.

Years later, when Facebook started, I got a hold of him—maybe forty years later?—and he wrote me back and told me he'd never forgotten me either. After that, we started talking on the phone every day, for three years, even though he could hardly breathe because he had emphysema and had to carry an oxygen tank. Every time Teenie called me, my heart would flutter like crazy.

Evidently Teenie had crushed on me the entire time I was in Memphis. Because Al got in the way, and later Shuggie, nothing romantic ever happened between me and Teenie—but in addition to that, I simply had no idea Teenie was interested. In 2013, Tennie came out to LA for a screening of a documentary about him, *Mabon "Teenie" Hodges: A Portrait of a Memphis Soul Original.* When we saw each other, it was like time had never ever escaped. We just looked at each other, like, "Damn." And he asked me, "How come you never liked me?"

I said, "I thought you liked Marquise!" Oh, well. That's where that ended. It was too late. Teenie had a damn oxygen tank with him, and he was very ill. It was rather hard to get together with anybody under those circumstances.

A year later, Teenie went to South by Southwest and played with Snoop Dogg, who I think smoked him out and killed him. That's a *joke*, of course. But I don't think it helped Teenie to be in a room full of all that smoke. That was his last gig. Right after the SXSW show, he was taken to Baylor hospital in Dallas for pneumonia, and he died three months later from complications of emphysema. I was devastated by Teenie's death and never got over it, but I was grateful that I at least got to reconnect with him after all that time. He meant so much to me. He still does.

I wonder what would've happened if I'd gone for Teenie back in the day. I might have married him and had a nice life in Memphis. But then I wouldn't be able to say I was with Al Green. With Al, my attitude was "okay, that's a one-night stand, that's a notch in my belt." But when it came to Teenie, I would have gotten seriously involved.

Mercy Fontenot *and* Lyndsey Parker

I might have fallen in love. And then I wouldn't have been with Shuggie, either. And then I wouldn't have my son, Lucky. However, I do sometimes wish I had gotten back in touch with Teenie before it was too late.

8

Lookin' for a Home

I WASN'T BACK IN LA for very long before I bolted again, this time on a road trip with my dad to Florida. My father was on a mission to rendezvous with this eighty-year-old Miami socialite, Marguerite, and convince her to marry him. It was obvious that my father only wanted this poor little old lady's money, but he was a car salesman, and apparently he was a very good one, because once he got to Florida he really sold her a bill of goods.

That entire trip was ridiculous. My dad was necking handfuls of diet pills and driving 100 miles an hour, and one time when he left his speed in a motel, he turned the car around and drove three hours in the reverse direction to retrieve it. Along the way, we stopped in New Orleans, which I insisted upon because my mother was a Fontenot, which made me half Cajun. That's when that psychic Gypsy told me there was no point in trying to outrun my destiny. "That guy that you're running away from, you're going to marry," she informed me.

My father had gotten very sick from all his amphetamine use, and now he, not Shuggie, was the one I really needed to escape from.

I was missing Shuggie so much it hurt, so I called him from Florida, not long after I arrived, and said, "I'm coming back."

Shuggie was waiting for me at LAX in his old Bonneville, and he told me, "Never leave me again!" Evidently I meant and mattered more to him than I'd thought. He drove me back to his place, and we became a real couple. I was with Shuggie for four years after that.

I lived in the Otis house for about two years before I got pregnant. I remember overhearing Johnny telling Shuggie, "If you keep screwing around with that woman, you're gonna knock her up." Johnny knew we were serious now, and that's what he was scared of, I guess. It's not that he didn't like me, but I didn't have money, any sort of nest egg, or solid family background. I was a drug addict and a GTO with a bad reputation.

I didn't get pregnant on purpose, I swear. I never schemed, never thought, "I'll get pregnant so Shuggie will be trapped into marrying me!" I just got pregnant through stupidity. I didn't keep track of my menstrual cycle. I never even thought about birth control. I was just dumb. But I was pretty excited to have Shuggie's baby, honestly. It would tie me to Shuggie for the rest of my life, which is what I wanted at the time.

I can't say Shuggie was delighted to be a father. He was young, about nineteen at this point, and I think he was confused more than anything else. It was a lot for him to process. He just accepted it. He never told me to get an abortion, nothing like that. Johnny and his wife, a wonderful saint of a woman named Phyllis, were ultimately happy—any grandchild addition, they would have been happy about—and they turned out to be stellar grandparents. Sure, Johnny might have warned Shuggie, "You're going to ruin your whole career," but to be honest, Johnny might've been right to think that. Shuggie was so sexy and popular and pretty. Being a husband and father probably hurt his heartthrob appeal.

During this time, Shuggie had another baby on the way: his long-gestating third album, *Inspiration Information*. It ultimately took him three years to finish it. That's twelve trimesters. Columbia Records kept ordering Shuggie to finish his album sooner than he wanted to, so he took his advance money and, as a big "fuck you" to Sony, used it to build a studio, Hawk Sound, in his family's backyard. Shuggie spent most of the time—and by that, I mean most of our relationship—cooped up in there. But I couldn't really be mad that he put his album first, before me and our child, because that would have been hypocritical of me. That's why I married Shuggie—because he was a musician! So I accepted it. In the long run, it was worth it. *Inspiration Information* has been brought up by everybody: Beyoncé, Raphael Saadiq, Lenny Kravitz, Prince. All of them took from that album. I knew when Shuggie was making it how important it was. But it came at a price.

Shuggie had a very bad reputation in the business by this point. Not only did he tell his record label to fuck off, but he actually turned down a chance to be in the Rolling Stones. Billy Preston called Johnny Otis about a Stones audition in France, and Johnny relayed the message to Shuggie, but Shuggie wasn't even remotely interested. "Forget it. I don't want to be with white boys." That's what he said.

"What the hell are you thinking?" I said. It really hurt his career, really screwed him up, because he became known as being irrational and eccentric and difficult. Which, frankly, he was. Billy Preston had a big crush on Shuggie and probably had ulterior motives for wanting Shuggie in the Stones, so that might have made Shuggie think twice. But I think, mainly, he did not want to be under anybody's control.

It wouldn't have worked, anyway. You can't put somebody as charismatic as Shuggie next to Mick Jagger. But it still would have been great to be a Stone's wife. And my mom would have been very excited to have her son-in-law be in the Rolling Stones. But it's

Mercy Fontenot *and* Lyndsey Parker

probably for the best that Shuggie said no. Being in a band with Keith Richards probably would have killed him within a couple of years, or even a couple of months. Nobody hangs out with Keith Richards, except for Ronnie Wood and Mick Jagger, and makes it out unscathed. Gram Parsons made it maybe a year and a half after meeting Keith. You have all this money and fame and everything, so what are you going to do? You're going to do a bunch of drugs, and you're going to try and keep up with Keith. And you're not going to make it. I know I wouldn't have.

Shuggie didn't really need the Stones anyway—when, thanks to his father, he had all the rock 'n' roll greats literally in his backyard. Of course his dad took advantage of Hawk Sound. His dad used it so much, in fact, that Shuggie had to book time in his own studio. Johnny helmed a record label called Blues Spectrum, and he'd bring everybody that started rock 'n' roll: Johnny "Guitar" Watson, Charles Brown, Eddie "Cleanhead" Vinson, Amos Milburn, Big Joe Turner, Louis Jordan. The absolute best. He had Ahmet Ertegun in there with Michael Stoller, Clarence "Gatemouth" Brown, Delmar "Mighty Mouth" Evans. Just having Big Joe Turner casually sitting in my living room was mind-boggling. I was constantly tripping out, surrounded by all this history. There were times when I just marveled to myself, "Oh, my God, oh, my God," over and over. "Oh, my God, these people started *everything.*"

I've talked about energy centers before. Hawk Sound was definitely one of them. Eventually, when Johnny and Phyllis moved to Altadena, Etta James, who lived catty-corner from the Otis house, told him, "I know somebody to sell it to"—and Johnny sold Hawk Sound to Alonzo Williams, from the World Class Wreckin' Cru, known as the Godfather of West Coast Hip-Hop. Dr. Dre and DJ Yella and all the Wreckin' Cru guys used that house as their home base in the mid-eighties, before NWA. It was truly a magical place.

I was well into my third trimester when I got a phone call from my mother saying, "Your father is in the hospital. He tried to kill himself again. You probably need to get over here." By the time I got there, Dad was gone.

For a few months before I married Shuggie, I'd lived with my father and his wealthy, elderly bride, Marguerite, in a posh apartment on Santa Monica's desirable Ocean Avenue. The Flames, these South African pop idols who had signed in America to the Beach Boys' American record label—and whose guitarist, Blondie Chaplin, I had a secret crush on—lived down the block. So did my mother, who'd divorced my father a few years before; my dad told Marguerite that my mom was his sister so she wouldn't be jealous.

The whole setup was weird. My father's octogenarian sugarmama was a raging alcoholic, so they had booze bottles stashed everywhere, even in the glove compartment of their Lincoln Continental. Marguerite slept in one bedroom, my dad in another. My father was tearing through Marguerite's money. If he was in a good mood, sometimes he'd buy me a few nice things. I'd go gambling with him and he'd have thousands of dollars in cash stuffed in his wallet. But eventually he drained that poor old bat's bank account and she kicked him out. Around that same time, his doctors cut off his shady prescriptions because the FDA was cracking down.

My father quickly lost everything. Creditors confiscated his fancy car, and he went to live with my mother because he literally had nowhere else to go. So he attempted suicide for the umpteenth time, while my mother was out working a night shift—and this time, he actually died. He did it with pills, of course; he had enough pills on his own, plus my mother, being a nurse, had plenty of pills stockpiled around her apartment. My dad had gotten all dressed up for the occasion, in his best suit. He must have been about fifty-eight.

My dad had been a suicide case many times, ever since the 1950s, but every time he had tried before, my mother would intervene and stop it. Not this time. My mother probably was glad in a way when my father was gone, because he really needed to go. He was just taking up space at this point, crashing on the couch in her cramped one-bedroom pad. My mother told me years later that when she came home that night and found my father, he was still breathing, but she just let him go.

When my dad died, I wasn't particularly distraught—or I didn't allow myself to be. My mom asked me to go to the hospital and get his wedding ring because she couldn't claim it since they were legally divorced by this point, but I didn't want to see him. I was just numb. Dad had disappeared out of my life so many times that this final vanishing act wasn't a big deal to me. And since I was pregnant at the time, it sort of felt that as one soul left the planet, another soul landed. My father checked out only a few days before my son Lucky was born.

I did feel some guilt, albeit fleetingly, because I'd sort of abandoned my father for Shuggie. Yes, our zany, speed-fueled Florida road trip had helped us get closer for a while, but Shuggie and I were on the phone to each other the entire time, and the minute I got the hint that Shuggie wanted me to come back, I bailed. My father was sick and he needed me, but I left anyway, and that was quite uncool of me.

I also wondered if the fact that I was having a Black man's baby had pushed my dad over the edge. My dad was a bit of a racist, or at least very white. He didn't appreciate any Black music. There was no Blackness to him. It was a very white world when I was growing up with him. I always got the sense that he didn't approve of me being with Shuggie. One of the final times I saw my father, when he brought some of my clothes over to the Otis house, he was behaving really strangely. His glum mood could have been the result of one of his amphetamine comedowns, or maybe it was because of the racial thing, but he was not acting like his usual charismatic, larger-than-life self.

When my father passed away, he left a bizarre goodbye letter on my mother's kitchen counter addressed to Rodney Allen Rippy (the child actor from the Jack in the Box commercials) and Morris the Cat. The last line of his suicide note read, "I had a great life."

Eventually I ditched the guilt because I knew my father would have gone out this way sooner or later. Suicide runs in my family, on both sides. When my sister was in the mental ward, she tried. My mom's brother, who was an alcoholic, took his life. My mother the pill-hoarder even used to morbidly announce that she had enough pills in the medicine cabinet to take out all four of us, if my family ever wanted to make some sort of group-suicide pact. I don't mean if doomsday was about to happen, like if an atomic bomb was about to go off—nothing that extreme. This was just Mom's backup plan if life ever got too tough. She actually used to say to me, "You know, you don't have much to live for. You might as well just take these pills." I guess my father eventually took her up on it, in a way. Later when my mom had breast cancer, she too died by suicide, Kevorkian-style, sort of a self-euthanasia thing.

I can't say I ever had suicidal tendencies, other than my silly, totally fake wrist-cutting stunt in the mental hospital as a teen. Once in a while I thought about jumping out a window, and there was this one time when I was in the car with my mother and was overcome by a crazy compulsion to grab the wheel and steer us over a cliff— but those were just weird flashes, and they soon passed. I always possessed a strong survival instinct and will to live, even though there were times when I thought, "God, it would be so much easier to be dead than to be in this situation." Then again, some people

Mercy Fontenot *and* Lyndsey Parker

might argue that my drug use was suicidal since I was well aware that I could die but didn't really care.

If I have to think of the main reason I never seriously contemplated suicide, it was Lucky. I think if I'd had nothing to live for, it might have been a different story. But soon I had him, and there was some kind of calling that I had to stay here, that I was supposed to remain on this planet to do something. It took me a while to figure out what that is. Lucky was a big part of it, but I also believe I was meant to stay here to relate to people in music—to be a communicator, a networker, a muse, whatever.

When it came time to give birth to Lucky, I went to the hospital by myself. I don't know where the fuck Shuggie was. I think he was recording; he had to have this album out by a certain deadline, and that was more important than my due date. I didn't experience any labor pains. The doctor gave me a saddle block, anesthetizing the hell out of me, and I couldn't feel a thing and didn't even have one contraction. The doctor induced labor, then there was the baby, the cutest little thing I'd ever seen. Lucky was born turned around, by the way. He was contrary and causing trouble even then, just like his dear old dad.

Shuggie finally came to the hospital a couple days later with Johnny, paid me a quick visit, and then went right back to recording. I recall I had my last name put on Lucky's birth certificate, and Shuggie screamed at me about that. But, hey, it could have been worse. I *was* going to name my son Jinx. I thought it was a cute name. But Johnny and Shuggie flipped their lids. Johnny said, "How could you do that? He'll be hexed for the rest of his life!"

So I said, "Fine, then, I'll call him Lucky." That's exactly how that happened.

Shuggie and I got married soon after Lucky was born. To me, it felt like we were already married; as long as I was in his house and in his bed every night, to me that was a marriage. But Phyllis, who was very traditional, told Shuggie, "Look, you cannot have the mother of your child living here in the house out of wedlock. You just don't do that. It's not right."

So Shuggie said to me, "Well, I have to marry you, so we're going to get married."

And I said, "Okay." That was our big, romantic, storybook proposal. I am sure he felt like he was being forced into it.

There was no big rock 'n' roll wedding. I didn't invite any friends. There was nobody there but my mother and a couple of Otis relatives. I went with my mother to Kmart to buy a silver dress beforehand and glued some blue rhinestones on it. We also drove around looking for a ring—it's not like Shuggie had gotten down on one knee with a diamond or anything—but we couldn't find one. Johnny, who was a preacher and was the leader of the Landmark Community Church in South Central LA, officiated the ceremony in the Otis house living room, probably very grudgingly. I don't recall what happened on our wedding night. We were probably doing cocaine, I hate to say it—our own idea of a white wedding. But I do remember that Shuggie went right back to his studio after we said "I do," literally the moment the ceremony was over. That was my honeymoon.

I probably should have been upset, but I wasn't because I was too wrapped up in Lucky by this point. Basically, Lucky became my obsession, which was typical behavior for a new mom, and *Inspiration Information* became Shuggie's. We were both distracted from each other. As much as that album came between us, Lucky came between us as well, because to me Lucky was my new world, just like that album was Shuggie's world. That's how everything started to go downhill. But Shuggie and I never talked about what was going wrong. I don't remember very many conversations at all after that, actually.

I believed Shuggie loved Lucky, and me, but he was not a good father. He was too young and too hyper-focused on his music and career. He also seemed bizarrely jealous of Lucky. Lucky was a beautiful little cherub of a boy. He could actually pass for Shirley Temple with his headful of adorable golden curls. But one day I went to the dentist and when I got home, at the top of the stairs Johnny was standing silently with Lucky. Lucky was completely bald. He had no hair. His curls were gone. Johnny whispered to me, "Don't say *anything*." So I walked in with my head hung low and kept my mouth shut, even though I was freaking out inside. Later I found out that Delmar "Mighty Mouth" Evans and Shuggie had been jamming together that day at the house and Lucky was crying and making a fuss, so Shuggie just chopped all of Lucky's hair off. I never mentioned it to Shuggie. I was too afraid of what he'd say if I asked him to explain.

Lucky almost drowned when he was a toddler. Apparently drowning runs in my family. And there was some divine intervention in this case, too.

Between the Otis house and Shuggie's studio ran a narrow bridge that led to a koi fishpond, next to a little office where Johnny kept a piano. I was in the house while Johnny and Shuggie were in the studio, and Lucky somehow crept out without me noticing. We had these wide windows that led to the backyard area and were never supposed to be opened, but they were unlocked that day. I remember that the God-like voice in my head—the one that had warned me "*don't do the drug deal*" back in San Francisco—echoed in my brain again. This time, it said, "*Get up*." Really loud, this big God voice. "*Get up. Go.*"

That's when I saw the worst thing I have ever seen: Lucky was floating in the koi pool, face-down. Thankfully, I could see a little bit of pink color in his flesh; if he would have been blue, I would have just lost my mind. I screamed like a banshee through the din of the recording session that was going on, and Johnny came racing out. Johnny pulled Lucky from the water and resuscitated him; I don't recall Shuggie doing anything.

After Lucky's accident, I spent all night in the hospital with him, alone. Shuggie stayed at Hawk Sound, recording. When Lucky and I came home later, though, this near-drowning incident did bring me and Shuggie closer for a while because I think we both realized what we might have lost. But, sadly, my dream was already too far on its way to being shattered.

I tried to leave Shuggie a couple times. Once I took off to San Francisco, but he followed me up there and retrieved me. I went up there with my old girlfriend Sapphire and her boyfriend, Blackbyrd McKnight. We were hanging with Johnny "Guitar" Watson, whom I crushed on, and I called Shuggie and threatened, "You'd better come get me"—implying that if he didn't, I'd go after Watson. Shuggie brought me home and told me, "Don't worry. You'll be here forever. You're not going anywhere." He wrote me a letter after that that read, "Don't ever leave me. I love you and Lucky the most." I found it on our bed. I wish I still had that letter.

Incidentally, Blackbyrd hit on me later, after I was separated from Shuggie and he was living with Sapphire. He showed up at my door out of the blue and said, "You know, I always had a thing for you."

I was like, "Okay, um...that's flattering. Bye!" I was not tempted. This was my ex-husband's good friend and my good friend's man, so I was not going to go there.

I did get to have a bit of input into Shuggie's album, which briefly made me feel like he and I were in this together and that this album was our baby too, so to speak. Shuggie told me the line "she moves the highs" in "Inspiration Information" was about me, and I in fact suggested that he name the album after that song. I even helped Shuggie with a bassline on "Inspiration Information." Still,

I felt increasingly sidelined. There may have been a great music scene happening in my own backyard, but I wasn't allowed to go be in the *outside* music scene. Shuggie wouldn't let me go out because he was too jealous. I was stuck in the best place I could be stuck in, Johnny Otis's house, watching all these brilliant musicians, and yet I still felt *stuck*. I felt like my whole life had been interrupted. *GTO, Interrupted* could have been the title of this book.

I couldn't do what I wanted to do. I couldn't be what I wanted to be. I felt like I was "Mrs. Shuggie Otis," and Mrs. Shuggie Otis had to act a certain way. Phyllis was the greatest wife in the world to Johnny, and she was an example of the kind of wife Shuggie expected: You cook, you stay home, you watch the kid, you clean up the rooms, you buy your housedresses at Kmart. You *behave*. But that was never me. I didn't know what that sort of marriage entailed. I didn't know anything about that kind of life. My parents were not exactly marital role models. Or parental role models, for that matter.

All of this really threw me. I had prayed so hard and for so long for my dream about Shuggie to come true—and then when it did, all I wanted was to go back to being myself and living my old life. I remember when I was doing our grocery shopping, I was in the supermarket checkout line, and on the cover of one of those gossip magazines the famous teenage groupies Lori Mattix and Sable Starr were saying the GTOs were "over the hill." Sable called us old bags: "The GTOs are over! We're the new ones!" I was only about twenty-five years old, but I didn't feel young anymore. I wanted some freedom. I wanted to go to clubs and feel young again.

And, on top of all this, Teri Wilson was still very much in the picture. While I was prioritizing Lucky, Shuggie was prioritizing his album, and then Teri, above me. So Shuggie was my number two, but I was Shuggie's number three or four. One night I came back early from visiting my mother and Shuggie was gone. He didn't come back until the next morning, when he drove up with Teri in the car. When he walked in the house, I just slapped the fuck out of him, right across the face. I didn't know what else to do. I was beyond distraught. Shuggie didn't say anything when I slapped him. He barely reacted at all. He expected it, I guess.

I've always thought that a song on Shuggie's second album from 1971, "Ice Cold Daydream," could be about me. It was certainly prophetic. A key line was, "You say that I'm a boy and we should part / So you can go and make a brand-new start." And then that happened.

I just ghosted Shuggie. That wasn't a term then, but ghosting is what I did. All I remember is getting in a cab with Lucky. I didn't even decide it. I just did it. I didn't sit there and think, "Maybe I'll leave him. Let me talk to the parents, let me talk to him. Let's talk it out, see a counselor, see a lawyer." I just picked up and took off running. Shuggie didn't try to stop me because he didn't know Lucky and I were leaving. But if he had known, I can't say he would have begged me to stay. Teri was waiting for him, and I knew that. I knew I had to step aside for Teri because that's the way this story was written. Shuggie may have been my dream, but the bottom line was I was not Shuggie's dream. *Teri* was his dream. So I left because I believed it was my fate to leave.

When it ended, I never tried to go back. I never called Shuggie, and he never called me. I never asked him if he wanted to get back with me, or if he thought about trying. I really didn't want to know the answer. There wasn't a chance to reconcile because Teri immediately swooped right in to take my place—or her rightful place, as it were. I also didn't go after Shuggie's money. Money wasn't why I'd married him, and it was not why I divorced him. What we had was never some sugar-daddy arrangement. So I didn't ask for any alimony or child support. I just wanted to block the marriage out of my life, and not be stuck seeing Shuggie every month. This was a major disservice to Lucky, I realize now. But Shuggie's career was careening downhill so rapidly, due to his bad reputation, that I probably wouldn't have gotten much anyway. And Shuggie was probably grateful that I had lessened his financial burden since he soon had a new wife, Teri, and a new son, Lucky's half-brother Eric, to care for.

Sometimes I allow myself to think back to a couple chance encounters when things could have been rekindled for us. The first time was when Johnny baptized Lucky in the Pacific Ocean. Afterward, I rode back to Johnny's church with him, and Shuggie was there. He and I had been split up for three years, with almost zero contact. Shuggie offered to drive me back to my place in Hollywood, much to my surprise. We got in the car and there was this deafening, awkward silence. Shuggie invited me to a recording session, but I politely declined. I actually think he might have been hitting on me. The second time, the Otis family was about to go on a trip to Santa Barbara and I ran into Shuggie and he invited me to join them. I think he was kidding that time, but who knows? I mean, he cheated on me with Teri, so why wouldn't he cheat on Teri with me? Sometimes I wonder what might have happened if I'd said yes either time, but I know that even if we had gotten back together in some way, it would have only been for one night.

I tried to maintain *some* sort of connection with Shuggie over the years, off and on, for Lucky's sake, but Teri and Shuggie ran hot and cold with me. It was like an on-and-off switch. Sometimes Teri could be friendly. She and I once went to see the Bar-Kays together—which made Shuggie seethingly jealous, of course, but we had a blast. Another fun time I had with the second Mrs. Shuggie Otis was when Shuggie played the Fairmont in San Jose when I was temporarily living up north with my sister. I ended up crashing in their hotel room, with both Shuggie and Teri. They had to bring a rollaway bed in. Shuggie cordially explained to the bellhop, "This is my wife, and this is my ex-wife."

But then there was the time when Johnny invited me and my mother to the Otis house, and when we showed up, Teri opened the door and screamed, "Get the fuck out of here! You don't belong here! What are you doing here?" She screamed so loud, she made my poor mother cry. And one time Teri called me in a rage and hissed into the receiver, "Now, listen to me: You don't know Shuggie. You *never* knew Shuggie. *Understand*?" I never could predict how Teri was going to act around me.

Shuggie and I did share a few sweet moments after our divorce. Once he called me out of the blue, and we talked for about eight hours that night. But then the next day he called me back and said, "Did you talk to Shuggie Otis last night?"—using the third person, strangely. I said, "Well, sure. At least I thought I did." And he said, "Nope, you didn't," and slammed down the receiver. I assume Teri put him up to that, but I don't know.

After Teri died, I did reach out to Shuggie. I knew he was hurting. I went over to visit him with Lucky, and when we got together, it was like no time had passed. We were laughing our asses off, just laughing and laughing, to the point where we almost forgot Lucky was there. We didn't mean to, but we hadn't seen each other in so long and we had so much catching up to do. Shuggie played me his new music, and I thought it was stupendous. We got along really, really swimmingly. Shuggie had recently gotten a big windfall from Beyoncé interpolating his hit song "Strawberry Letter 23," so he offered to take me and Lucky shopping. He bought me a limited-edition Band album for ninety dollars, and he bought Lucky a $3,000 computer. It was really quite sweet. That was a lovely day.

Shuggie and I also had a very emotional Facebook conversation many years later, when he wrote me out of nowhere—I think maybe he'd heard that I'd been ill—to tell me, "You're a winner!" He described what we'd had as a "pure love," and he told me, "I'll always love you and Lucky."

I wrote back, "You're a winner too. You've always been a winner. I'll always love you too. I want you to know that you are the person I loved the most."

The last time I saw Shuggie in person was at his mother Phyllis's memorial in 2016. I only talked to him for a moment; for some reason I seized up, became uncharacteristically shy, and bolted. I simply didn't know how to deal with it, didn't know how to console him in his grief. I really regret not finding the right words to say that day.

I don't think I'll ever have total closure with Shuggie. To have that, we'd need another face-to-face chat, not random texts or Facebook messages. I want to believe that I will probably see him again in my lifetime—or, if not, in another lifetime. Otherwise, he and I are going to have lifetimes of unfinished business.

When I look back on my favorite memories of my marriage to Shuggie, it's never anything "romantic." It's not our first date, or our first kiss, or the first time we went to bed together, and it's certainly not our shotgun wedding. It's all the sessions in our backyard, or a Muscle Shoals session Shuggie and I attended with Fayne Pridgon and Ahmet Ertegun, or a show in Oakland that Shuggie played with T-Bone Walker and Robin Ford. It's Shuggie's session out in Mill Valley with Buddy Miles, Al Kooper, and Mike Bloomfield, or it's Bo Diddley's London Sessions with Johnny Otis producing and me and one of my soul idols Clydie King doing coke in the bathroom.

One of the highlights of my life, truly, was witnessing those London Sessions. I said to Bo, "What sign are you?"

And he answered without missing a beat, "I'm the devil, baby!" Evidently Bo was a Capricorn, but that was really cool. Those were the best of times, which more than made up for the worst of times.

Sure, sometimes I wish Shuggie and I could have lived happily ever after. When I see a photograph of him or hear his music or when he writes or calls me, I still react to it, viscerally. It tears me apart. It's so tempting to speculate about what could have been, what would have been, what should have been, if Teri hadn't come into the picture (or hadn't existed), or if I'd stuck it out and tried to make it work. But then, I wouldn't be the person I am today. I wouldn't be Miss Mercy. I would just be Mrs. Shuggie Otis.

9

Only the Strong Survive

(Trigger warning: sexual assault and battery)

THE ONLY THING THAT ever really traumatized me in my entire life was when I was with Shuggie and he got in multiple car accidents with me along for the ride. I had to jump out of a lot of cars during our marriage. As I've mentioned, Shuggie had serious jealousy issues, and his main weapon when we were fighting was to slam his foot down on the accelerator and get angrier and angrier. For some reason he would start grilling me about whom I'd slept with in the past, and there was no way for me to answer without enraging him. Sometimes he'd work himself into such a frenzy that I would swing open the car door and bail, just leap out like some kind of a stuntwoman.

One time Shuggie smashed into this poor woman's car; thankfully she wasn't injured, but she told us, "I just lost my son a year ago, to this very day, in a car accident." My heart sank. From that point on, my mind was so mangled that I could never get behind the wheel of an automobile ever again. Even when I was sitting in the front, in the passenger seat, I'd envision car crashes that hadn't even happened yet. I could never sit back and relax. I was totally tensed up for fifteen years. I was so scared of getting killed in a car crash that

I just couldn't deal with it. That's the most traumatic thing that ever happened to me.

Getting raped multiple times, however, didn't actually traumatize me that much.

Maybe in my subconscious, part of my lack of interest in sex comes from being sexually assaulted so many times. I've gone to bed with rock stars who were bona fide sex symbols, and you'd think the sex with them would be mind-blowing, but sometimes it was quite the opposite. Then again, I think a lot of those rock stars probably just didn't feel like they had to make much effort. After all, countless groupies were happy to go to bed with these guys no matter what—and if these chicks didn't get satisfaction, so what? There were plenty of other girls willing and eager to service these men, no shortage of interchangeable, disposable partners. So, maybe a guy who felt like he didn't have as many opportunities to get laid would have made more of an effort to please.

Anyway, the first time I was raped, I was hitchhiking in San Francisco. I was sixteen. I got in the car, the guy drove under a bridge, stopped, and raped me. And then he drove me back to where he'd found me. That was it. That's all that happened. I complied because I wanted to live. I told myself, "Just do what he says and shut the fuck up."

Then there was the time when I went out clubbing in San Francisco with my on/off boy toy, Reggie from the Cockettes, and this guy told me he had some heroin. So, like an idiot, I abandoned Reggie and went off with this stranger to a motel room. When the dude shut the door, he started heating up a frying pan. It turned out there wasn't any heroin at all. He told me, "I'm gonna pour this hot grease on you if you don't fuck me." So, yes, I totally fucked him. His next-door neighbor came in moments after it was all over, but I didn't feel like I could say a damn thing.

However, those were minor incidents, in my mind, compared to what happened to me down in Hollywood.

There was one LA evening when my gal pal and I were hitchhiking on our way to go dancing at a gay club, and this studious, very normal-looking guy picked us up. I didn't get any sort of bad vibes from him. My friend and I squeezed into the front seat together. But then our driver decided to pick up two men at a bus stop. They got in the back seat, and all of a sudden I felt something on the back of my head. It was a gun. One of the men in the back told the driver, "I want you to keep driving, or I'm going to blow her head off." The driver obeyed, seeming as freaked out as we were. Being accustomed to jumping out of cars, I considered pushing my friend out the door, but we were on the freeway by this point, so she most certainly would've gotten killed.

The guys claimed they were George Jackson's brothers. George Jackson was this activist who'd been serving a sentence for armed robbery since 1961 and was the cofounder of the Black Guerrilla Family. It was this big political thing that was going on, and these guys said they wanted to get him out of a courtroom, or something like that, so they were going to take us as hostages. As it turned out, George's seventeen-year-old brother, Jonathan, did later ambush a Marin County courtroom with an automatic weapon to free some other prisoners known as the Soledad Brothers—this was national news. But I don't know to this day if Jonathan was one of the guys in the car with us.

These men came up with the bright idea to rape us before going to the courtroom, so we made a pit stop in an abandoned building. I don't really have any gory details. They didn't hold us down, or threaten us, and we didn't try to escape. We just got on our backs and let them do what they were determined to do, taking turns, because they had a gun. The only way to get out of that kind of situation, meaning not get killed, was to play the game. So I was accepting of the circumstances and hoped I would survive it. And I'd rather it be this than some bigger scene, like getting gunned down in a courthouse.

When it was all over, the guys began rummaging through our purses, but there was no light in the house, so they went outside to look under the porch lamps, taking our handbags with them—and they expected the driver, who'd been there all along, witnessing all of this, to follow them. But at that point, the driver tried to make a run for it. Our kidnappers shouted, "Oh, no, there's our ride!" and followed him—and just left us behind.

We didn't report it. Back then—and not that much has changed, unfortunately—the rape victim was always the guilty one. First of all, the cops would have turned it into a Black-and-white issue. And second, the cops would have grilled us: "What were you doing? What were you wearing? Why were you hitchhiking?" So, we went back to hitchhiking. We found another ride, made it to the gay club, and danced our cares away for the rest of the night.

These supposed Jackson dudes seemed to have a political mindset going into our attack, so I know this sounds weird and might not make any sense, but they weren't that scary to me. I understood their political motivations. They weren't being really brutal about it; it was just like something that they had to do, almost something they had to get out of the way, before they embarked on their real mission. Maybe they knew that was their last time they would do anything sexual. I didn't feel threatened by them the way I would by the men who perpetrated my second LA rape.

That time, another girlfriend of mine and I were down in the Crenshaw district, in front of a liquor store, and we met this older guy who had some angel dust and went back with him to his house. Yes, we did some really dumb things back then. The man had some younger friends there, and I remember that Michael Jackson's "I'll Be

Scaring the Easter Bunny as a young girl, 1950s.

With my sister, Sandra, at the beach shortly before my first near-death experience, 1958.

With Miss Cynderella in the studio, 1968. (Image courtesy of Zappa Trust)

A moment of reflection in the studio with the GTOs, 1968. (Image courtesy of Zappa Trust)

With my dear Jobriath, late sixties. (Photo: Frank Aqueno)

With Ricky Klampert, ready for my close-up on the set of Otto Preminger's Skidoo, *1968.*

With Pamela Des Barres and Ricky Klampert at Marlon Brando's house, 1968. (Photo: Andee Nathanson)

Having my cake and throwing it too, high on angel dust at Alice Cooper's "Coming Out Party" at the Ambassador Hotel on Bastille Day, 1971. (Photo: Noel Brooks / Courtesy of Fairchild Archives)

A glamour headshot from my short-lived actress days.

Modeling Shuggie's hat, early seventies.

My "Rayvee Raveon" era, early eighties.

ROLLING STONE

FEBRUARY 24, 1968
VOL. I, No. 6

OUR PRICE:
TWENTY-FIVE CENTS

ACME

MONTEREY FESTIVAL ON AGAIN; ROME SHOW OFF

It Happened In 1967

For the ROLLING STONE AWARDS and first annual "Look Back In Anger" review of the year past, see Page 11. Janis Joplin, a winner, is shown above; a scene from the Gathering of the Tribes, another winner, below.
PHOTOGRAPHS BY BARON WOLMAN

Adler Given First Shot at Fairgrounds

BY MICHAEL LYDON

The Monterey International Pop Festival is going to happen again—maybe, and — m a y b e again—the F e s t i v a l will soon have straightened out the financial mess left after M o n t e r e y 1967.

Festival producer Lou Adler has spoken with George Wise, manager of the Monterey County Fairgrounds where the first festival was held, and asked that the grounds be tentatively reserved for June 21, 22, 23. Adler, who ran last year's Festival with John Phillips, has been unreachable, but friends say he is enthusiastic about the prospect of another one.

But so far no staff has been hired, and since first speaking with Wise early in January, Adler has done nothing to confirm the dates. "All he has to do is call," says Wise. "I liked working with Adler's group last year, and I am giving them first priority. But they will have to speak soon."

Adler has to decide because Charles Royal, publisher of Roy-

—Continued on Page 4

Rome 'Festival' Turns Out to Be Small Time Job

Out of the murk of small time promoters came the name of the "First International European Pop Festival," and back into the murk it has slipped, perhaps never to be heard from again. Originally planned for February, it has been postponed to May and may never come off at all.

The Festival, which had a letterhead, a few representatives in various capitals and, so says rumor, a pair of rich Americans and an Italian prince behind it, was scheduled for February 19 through 25 at Rome's Palazzo dello Sport. Over a dozen English groups were claimed to have signed, Country Joe and the Fish did sign a contract, and other American (mostly San Francisco) groups agreed to appear pending signing of contracts.

But late in January groups which had agreed got terse telegrams signed "First International European Pop Festival." The telegrams read: "Festival set back May-June; Sicilian disaster; delayed American acceptances; requests for delay for more widespread international representation; publicity; and backer's orders. Festival will happen. New

BOB DYLAN COMES OUT AT WOODY MEMORIAL

BY SUE C. CLARK

NEW YORK

Bob Dylan finally emerged from 18 months of self-imposed seclusion at the Woody Guthrie Memorial Concert in Carnegie Hall on January 20. His appearance had b e e n announced and the two performances were sold out weeks in advance. Scalpers

sidewalk and in the lobby begging, "Extra tickets? Any tickets for sale?"

In addition to Dylan, the memorial concert also featured Pete Seeger, Judy Collins, Woody's son Arlo Guthrie, Tom Paxton, Jack Elliot, Odetta and Richie Havens, all performing songs written by Guthrie. Before and after each song, Robert Ryan, the program's narrator, and Will Geer did readings from Guthrie's work, accompanied by slides and

resplendently dressed. O d e t t a wore an orange and gold striped floor-length caftan, Judy Collins sported a red rose at the neck of her long-sleeved white blouse, while Richie Havens had on a purple silk Indian shirt beneath a black Nehru suit with a long jacket. But Bob Dylan, in a gunmetal grey silk mohair suit, blue shirt with green jewels for cuff links and black suede boots as well as his new beard and moustache, was the center of atten-

With my closest friend Cinnamon Muhlbauer in Rona Barrett's gossip column, 1981.
(Photo: George Rodriguez)

With my beloved Lucky.

Rare family reunion with Shuggie and Lucky Otis.

*Modeling flashy fashions
with Pamela Des Barres
and my father,
late sixties.*

*My enigmatic father with
Ann-Margret, 1970.*

Actress Bethany Ziskind, a dead ringer for me, in the stage production Shock Opera. *(Photo: Julia Reodica)*

With fabulous RuPaul's Drag Race *winner Bianca Del Rio. (Photo: Lyndsey Parker)*

With Anthony Kiedis and my dear Steve Olson, mid-2000s.

Reuniting with the wonderful Teenie Hodges in 2013. (Photo: Cinnamon Muhlbauer)

With Exene Cervenka of X, Shirley Manson of Garbage, and Lyndsey Parker at X's fortieth anniversary celebration.

With Alana and Este Haim of HAIM, 2018. (Photo: Brad Elterman)

With the stunning Alexa Chung at her "The Muse" collection launch party, 2018. (Photo: Brantley Gutierrez)

With Arrow de Wilde of Starcrawler, 2018. (Photo: Brad Elterman)

With my coauthor and guardian angel, Lyndsey Parker, at Alexa Chung's "The Muse" party, 2018.
(Photo: Brantley Gutierrez)

With Rodney Bingenheimer and Dave Davies as Dave's invited guest, backstage at the Roxy, 2015.
(Photo: Rebecca G. Wilson)

With Pamela, my best friend of many lifetimes. (Photo: Daniel Vega-Warholy)

Outtakes from my cover shoot for Starcrawler's single "She Gets Around." (Photos: Gilbert Trejo)

There" was playing on the stereo. I'll never forget that it kept playing over and over and over, after things started up.

I thought the younger guys were kind of cute. I was sitting with a couple of them in the kitchen, just hanging out, when all of a sudden I heard a big thump coming from the living room. Somebody had kicked my girlfriend in the head. That was when everything switched.

These guys dragged my friend into one bedroom while they dragged me into another room. And more guys showed up—continually, more and more came. They were Crips gang members, though the Crips were not talked about at that time—around 1969 or 1970. I don't even know if they were widely known as the Crips yet. But they told us, "We're the Crips, and if you don't know who we are, you will know now. We're your worst nightmare."

More and more men kept coming in, until about six in the morning. I literally do not know how many dudes raped me, or how many times. It was a train that kept on going. At one point I got real smartass with one of them and said something like, "Would you do this to your wife?" I really was just pissed, to tell you the truth.

The guy fucking slapped me hard across the face and shouted, "I'll kill you, you bitch!" These gang members were a lot different than those supposed Jackson brothers; the Jacksons, even though they'd put a gun to our heads, hadn't been violent like *this*. These monsters, when they were raping me, kept calling me a "dumb white bitch" over and over.

So I was lying there, thinking, "How do I get out of this? They're going to fucking kill us." Because we knew where they lived, so they'd be scared to let us out the door. Not knowing what else to do, I hit on the older gang leader that was running the whole show. I flirted with him: "I'm sick of all these high school kids! These young guys don't know anything about sex. I want to sleep with you, I want to be with you. You're so handsome. *You're* the one I want to be with!" And he bought it. He took me into the bedroom, and I stayed with him and pleasured him until he gathered up me and my friend and drove us home. He actually drove us to my house, which was pretty stupid of me because now he knew where I lived. But that was the last of it.

And, no, I didn't report this case either. I was not going to call the police and say, "I just got raped by the Crips." Once again, they would have said, "What were you doing there? It's your fault." And I would have understood why they said that, frankly. I'm not saying I blame myself for what happened, on any of the occasions when I was assaulted, or that I deserved it or "asked for it." I'm just saying that I shouldn't have been in those places to begin with. I put myself in some shady situations. Plus, I was worried that if I called the police, I'd end up indicted on drug charges.

So, I just got over it, over and over again. We didn't have AIDS or herpes or any incurable STDs at that time—nothing really floating around except syphilis, which a doctor could get rid of—so it was a different thing. And I didn't get pregnant, so that was great. I was just happy to survive. My logic was, if I get out of it alive, once I'm out, it's over and done.

I had sort of a Joan of Arc mindset—like, I could deal with this, because I had God behind me. I was able to take the fall for women who couldn't take it. Whoever would have been raped instead of me, I'm the one that got put in her place because I could handle it. I just accepted it, like a martyr: better me than somebody else who'd end up psychologically screwed up for the rest of her life.

It is possible that I have a stronger will or survival skills than some people. There are people who've been through much less than me who cannot move on from their PTSD. Maybe I'm just in denial about my trauma. But then again, if I were in denial, I wouldn't admit it.

10

The New World

THE FIRST TIME I HEARD what would now be described as punk music was in 1969, at the world-infamous Wilton Hilton, a dilapidated Hollywood duplex that looked like something out of *The Addams Family*. The Wilton Hilton later became the home base for bands like Blondie and the Screamers, and it was featured on the cover of the Cramps' *Psychedelic Jungle* album, but long before that, it was known for being a hub for the occult. There were stories about bones buried in the backyard—those were dead stray cat bones, which had nothing to do with anything, but I do believe that the place was haunted. And that is because back when I was living there, with Sapphire and another girl who was supposedly a witch, I ventured down to the basement, and Sapphire and this guy Greg and Donna Bates were playing this crazy, creepy music—if it could even be called that—in a group called Doris, Boris & Dolores.

This was punk before punk became punk. It sounded like twenty years ahead of punk—either that or it was abstract jazz, one of the two. Heavy metal abstract jazz? Whatever it was, it was totally out-there. The cacophony emanating from that basement sounded like nothing I'd ever heard before and like nothing I ever wanted to hear again. It sounded like a nightmare to me—like the sound itself was haunted. I didn't know where it came from—I thought it came from hell, to tell you the truth. It scared me to death. "My God, what is that? It's really actually horrifying," I told them. Soon after that, I ended up leaving the Wilton Hilton and moving in with Shuggie. I think I was terrified. I wasn't ready yet.

Years later, I went over to the Wilton Hilton to visit my old room, and Tomata du Plenty from the notorious, short-lived punk group the Screamers was now occupying it. So that house just held punk. I think punk came out of that house; I really do. Somebody let it out of the basement.

It was years before I got into punk myself, albeit sort of accidentally and begrudgingly. I was twenty-seven by then, living with my mother most of the time, and I already felt like my best days were behind me. My mom was always putting it in my head that I was "over the hill" and a failure. "What are you going to do with your life?" she would ask me. I suppose it was a valid question, but she did a lot of psychological damage. I realize now that she was just projecting her insecurities onto me because she was getting older too. Anyway, it felt strange being single and venturing out into Hollywood again. I had no idea what twenty-seven meant in the real world. The LA punk scene skewed so much younger, like sixteen or seventeen, and it was hard for me to get back into the teenage swing of things. But I knew this was where I needed to be.

It all started when my old friend Marlowe B. West introduced me to a girl named Shannon Wilhelm—a ballerina who was also in a punk band called Castration Squad and lived at another run-down, punk-rock flophouse apartment building, the Canterbury, which was home to members of the Go-Go's, the Germs, and some of the Screamers. Oh, man, I had such a crush on Shannon. Weeks later

I crashed in bed with her and I started to feel her up. She said, "No, no, we're not going to do that."

So that didn't work out. But we eventually became close friends, and it was Shannon who introduced me to the legendary punk club the Masque, run by a Scottish visionary named Brendan Mullen. The fateful evening I ran into her at Marlowe's place, she took one look at me and said, "Come on. Let me take you somewhere."

Shannon led me down into this scary den of iniquity, downstairs in a decaying building on a dark Hollywood side street. I will never, ever forget the first time I went there. It seemed against every hippie thing I ever believed in. I descended into that basement and saw "kill hippies" graffiti scrawled in what looked like blood all over the walls. I didn't know what I was getting into. Punk was already looking very odd to me. But the vibe was there. That special energy was something I recognized. The Masque was bizarre and scary, but I had to be there because of that energy. The former Masque is now the headquarters for World of Wonder, the company that created *RuPaul's Drag Race*, so I believe that building is still special and powerful.

Next, Don Bolles from the Germs took me to see the Consumers' first gig at the Whisky, and I was going, "Oh, my dear Lord, look at this place. It looks like shit." The Whisky was tore up from the floor up and didn't look like anything like the elegant place I'd once known. The Consumers were onstage trying to strangle their lead singer— which I thought was a joke at first, but it wasn't a joke. Apparently all the band members hated him and they genuinely wanted to murder him. Then Black Randy & the Metrosquad hit the stage and totally mangled a James Brown song, which to me was fucking insulting and downright blasphemous. I was thinking, "Jesus, how ugly can this get? How bad can this get? There's no bridge, it's just four chords and evil thoughts. This isn't even music."

After being so isolated with Shuggie for years at the Otis house, where I'd seen all the rock 'n' roll greats and the origins of soul and R&B and blues, to come out of hiding and walk into the Masque or Whisky and hear all this fucked-up, violent, raging noise was a shock to my system. It was just too much for me, but I could not stay away. I knew something important was happening—something that I wanted to get rid of, to be honest. I decided I was going to change the scene from within, like some sort of punk-rock double agent.

I wanted to put some funk into the punk. I spent all my time trying to educate these young punk people. I would tell them, "You're playing shit. What are you doing? This is shit. Listen to *this*." I talked to a lot of the people, a lot of the punk girls, about the blues, and sometimes I changed their perspective. I worked really hard at doing this. I wasn't doing it for a dollar; I was doing it more for the feeling of, "Oh, wow, I did something good. Down the road, this will be an important thing that I did." For instance, I remember being over at X's house with Belinda Carlisle, and I handed Belinda a list of Black songs that I thought the Go-Go's should cover, and one of them was "Cool Jerk" by the Capitols. They ended up recording it a few years later.

Penelope Spheeris asked me to be in her ground-breaking Los Angeles punk documentary, *The Decline of the Western Civilization, Part 1*, which would have furthered my cause. I had a master plan: I was going go there with my *T.A.M.I Show* book and open it to the page with James Brown and say to the camera, "Listen, I don't know what you all think that you're doing, but *this* is what really matters." But I never got to do that. I was so high on speed that I couldn't find the Slash Records building where Penelope's crew was shooting, so I missed that boat.

One night at the Whisky, I finally found my kindred spirits, my allies in my noble mission. In strutted this amazing-looking group of rockers with their manager Leee Black Childers, who'd worked at

Andy Warhol's Factory and at David Bowie's management company, MainMan. These guys had fantastically styled pompadours, and I immediately exclaimed to them, "Oh, thank God you're here, what a relief! Who are you? You're my dream haircuts!"

And Leee told them, "This is Mercy! Do you *know* who Mercy is?" Of course they didn't. Leee said to them, "Oh, man, if you only *knew* who this woman is!"

The band was Levi & the Rockats, and they would soon become everything to me. The Rockats were crossing punk over to rock 'n' roll, rockabilly, soul—you know, *real* music. But when the lead singer, Levi, first opened his mouth, he had a British accent, which annoyed me. I didn't like the English in the first place because I thought bands like the Beatles had stolen the thunder of American musicians, the soul musicians, who were the originators. I said, "Oh, my God, *why* did you have to be English? You had to be English to bring American music back to America again." It felt like the 1960s British Invasion all over again. But the Rockats were ready to revive rockabilly in the mid-seventies. So I flat-out told them, "We've already had this kind of music here. But, hey, it's great that you're doing this because we need to hear it again." Whatever the hell I'd been hearing in the punk clubs was plenty frightening, and this was a much better option. So I became friends with the Rockats and started doing their hair.

I only did hair to get in with the punk scene, and because I could never deal with doing normal work. It was really all part of my secret scheme to fight *against* the punk scene. I did what I could do, and I'm happy with what I did. I became known as Rayvee Raveon—the name was a mix of Revlon and "Rave On" by Buddy Holly. I enrolled in beauty school and started styling all the punks in town. *Eraserhead* was a big inspiration for my hairstyle creations, along with James Dean and African American hairstyles of the fifties and sixties. I called my signature style the "Spiked Rockabilly," and I bleached everybody this translucent, luminescent blonde. Luminize was my favorite Clairol product on the planet; I put it in everything, on everyone. Some people started changing the way they looked, as well as the music they liked, so I believe I had an influence.

My main hair thing was a sky-high pompadour because I was inspired by Black people's hair. I actually got in trouble at my Santa Monica hair school over that. The head lady was racist, and she did not want me to do Black hairstyles. She would never give me a chair to practice in. I had enrolled in night classes to get away from her, actually. I wanted to get her fired over this. One day, I was summoned to the principal's office and he told me, "We have a bunch of people that are protesting our head teacher, but nobody will say anything. Will you go to court and say what you have to say?" I readily agreed, and on Halloween day I dressed up Lucky as Devo and took him into the courtroom with me.

I was all dressed up as a member of KISS, I forget which one— later that day Lucky and I actually won his school's mother/child costume contest. So I sat there in the courtroom in my KISS costume and stated, "This lady is very prejudiced. She won't let me do a pompadour on Black people." They ended up putting the case in the newspaper, and she did, in fact, get fired.

Still, it was time for me to relocate to the Hollywood Boulevard hair school, right next to Frederick's, where I would clearly fit in better. I made the whole window display there punk, and brought in punk hairstyles, and all the teachers loved me. They thought I was inspiring and someone to watch.

Meanwhile, I was hanging with the Rockats, and I really wanted to make Levi's American dream come true. The first thing he'd said to me when he met me at the Whisky was, "I want to go to Shreveport and play the *Louisiana Hayride*," a longstanding, legendary country music TV show. And with the help of my friend

Tom Ayres, this actually came to pass. Tom, who was from Louisiana, was the guy who'd famously brought David Bowie to RCA Records and had cofounded Rodney's English Disco with Bowie and Rodney Bingenheimer. Tom had once offered to introduce me to Bowie, and Bowie had wanted to meet me in the GTOs days, but Bowie's glam trip wasn't my thing. Instead, I asked Tom to let me meet Gene Vincent, who was recording at Tom's place. Later, when Tom brought an unknown folk singer named Victoria Williams to LA from Louisiana, I was the first person that Victoria met, and I got her a spot in Johnny Otis's church choir. (She was white, yes, and Johnny accepted her.) So anyway, I got in touch with Tom, and Tom made sure that the Rockats got their ride on the *Hayride*. I ended up going with them, watching these English blokes playing rootsy punk in the middle of Shreveport, having the time of their lives. It was really quite funny.

My hairstyling work for the Rockats caught the eye of another big guy in the scene, Kidd Spike of the Gears. He saw how fantastic the Rockats looked and asked me, "Oh, God, can you do my hair too?" And then I ended up being the Gears' stylist and going everywhere with them. I went to thrift stores and got them their clothes, and Spike made my big quiff iconic. I did sleep with one of the other Gears, once—the bassist, Brian Redz. He had a girlfriend at the time. I don't know if he remembers that night, but I do. It was just cute, and I have fond memories of it. But I always had a major unrequited crush on Kidd Spike.

The Gears played genuine rock 'n' roll music, not punk. They had a real sound to them. There were certain other groups that had roots, like the Cramps, and of course X, whose guitarist Billy Zoom was a rockabilly veteran who'd actually played with Gene Vincent and Etta James. Top Jimmy & the Rhythm Pigs were another one. Top Jimmy, who is sadly gone now, could sing like Merle Haggard meets Howlin' Wolf meets Jim Morrison, and he was absolutely incredible to behold.

Van Halen even wrote a song about him and called him the "baddest cat alive." The scene was shifting, much to my delight, and I started hanging at another punk institution, the Cathay de Grande. It was a dump and it smelled like death, but to me it was the best scene in the world. It was more integrated, and the bands there, like Los Lobos, the Alley Cats, and the Blasters, were dead-serious musicians, unlike most of the other noisy punks. I liked the Cathay de Grande so much that I even took my old friend Delmar "Mighty Mouth" Evans there as part of my mission to educate the punk kids.

The Blasters were another big band for me. Brothers Phil and Dave Alvin came from an R&B/rockabilly background and used to hang at the Ash Grove when they were teenagers, so they were the perfect punk soldiers to draft for my mission. I was nuts over the Blasters, and so thankful for them. We just became like brothers and sister, very close. One night Phil gave me a ride home and then we had a small sexual encounter. Well, he wasn't *small*, if you catch my drift. Anyway, we had an oral adventure, but that was a one-time thing because he had a girlfriend. Many years later I said to Phil, "Do you remember what happened back in the day?"

And he said to me, "Yes, I was with a GTO and it kind of freaked me out." It turned out he and his brother Dave had been big GTOs fans and had even attended the Shrine Auditorium show.

Most of the young punks didn't know about my past before I was "Rayvee Raveon." Nobody even knew who the GTOs were. Even if they had known, it would have meant nothing to them because punk was all about rejecting everything of the past. And let's face it, twenty-seven years old was ancient to most of these people. The LA scene had rapidly changed. I remember the night that Robert Plant came to the Starwood to see Michael Des Barres play...and the club wouldn't let him in. They had no idea who Robert was because it was during the punk era. "You guys are *nuts*," I told them.

But some of the punks, like the Blasters, or Don Bolles, who proudly owned the GTOs album, were aware of my legacy and respected it. When I was an extra in the Ramones' movie *Rock 'n' Roll High School* (I was in the concert scene at the Roxy; if you look real closely, in the hallway I'm the one with the blond hair and red leopard-print forties dress), Dee Dee Ramone, who'd dated Connie Gripp, was right next to me. I looked at Dee Dee and said, "Hey, I'm Mercy from the GTOs."

And he flipped out and exclaimed, "Oh, my God, you *are*? I have your album. It cost me like five hundred bucks!"

There weren't that many Black people in the punk scene, but one night at the second Masque—after the first Masque was shut down—Brendan Mullen booked a Black band just for me. "Here's something for Mercy! I finally found her some soul brothers!" he announced merrily. And then he brought up this all-Black punk group called Pure Hell. I'm not sure if Brendan was kidding or not. I am sure he meant well, but this noise was *not* the sort of Black music that turned me on, and I felt an urgent compulsion to flee because I was super high and the place seemed to start burning, like I was literally trapped in pure hell. Fires were blazing in my mind. But that's how I met the famous, number-one skateboarder Steve Olson. I ran out of the Masque in terror, and this gorgeous guy drove up in this nice car, saw me in distress, and offered me a ride. We became very close pals after that. I got Steve into rockabilly, basically. He had long hair, so I started spiking it, and together we started injecting the punk look in the skateboarding scene.

Brendan later started booking a great venue called Club Lingerie, where he brought in all New Orleans music and R&B because that was his favorite thing. Brendan didn't start the Masque to start punk; that just happened. He and I bonded over R&B and got along amazingly well. One evening I was over at his place doing his hair, and we ended up in bed together. It was the most incredible sex I've ever had in my life. Brendan was really great at fucking, simple as that. A lot of men didn't do oral stuff, or it was in-and-out, but Brendan knew what he was doing. I finally realized that something magical can happen when you have a physical encounter with somebody. I thought, "Wow, this is fun. This is good. This works. This may be what it's all about." I hadn't felt that way with a man ever before, not even Shuggie. You have to realize that when I was with Shuggie, he was a kid, so what did he know about sex? And what did I really know? I didn't know a whole lot, to be honest. Sex did not rule my world.

My tryst with Brendan was only a one-time thing. We didn't carry on an affair, because he had a lot of affairs. Brendan was a whore, what can I say? He was very popular and slept with a lot of people. But one time was enough for me. I am loathe to call it a one-night stand because I truly respected Brendan. I just didn't need to spoil the memory by being with him again. I got my fill and checked that box. I mean, it doesn't get any better than that, so why do it again?

My other all-time best sexual experience was with Jerry Sikorski, the guitarist from Ray Campi & the Rockabilly Rebels. I went to his house one night and didn't go home for three days. Jerry and I had had sex for seventy-two hours straight. Oh, man, he was really good at it. He and Brendan were the two people that made me realize sex could be an awesome thing. But most of the time, it wasn't. I just did it to put a notch in my belt, like with Al Green. It didn't have to be this mind-blowing experience.

Hollywood Joe, a.k.a. Joe Nania, was another punk-era "boyfriend" of mine. I wasn't really having a relationship with him, but we were going to bed together during an affair that was off and on for about five years. The sex was pretty good; Joe was merely so beautiful to look at. Just looking at him made me melt. Hollywood Joe was the finest-looking man I've ever seen in my whole life, the most handsome guy on the planet. He looked just like Victor Mature. He was the doorman of the Troubadour but also played jazz guitar, and Tom Ayers eventually started to produce him.

I also had an affair with Spider, the lead singer of a punk band called the Red Army, who sometimes worked as a bodyguard at the Masque. Well, we had *sort* of an affair, but he was really in love with a girl named Danger. That's how it went back then. But Spider actually lived with me for three or four months in an apartment on Vine Street across from Ranch Market. When the Red Army first came out from Arizona, I dyed all of the band members' hair fire-engine red, and they tried to gain notoriety in the LA scene by bragging that they were going to beat the shit out of Darby Crash of the Germs. Spider made good on that threat and jumped Darby onstage, or something like that, and he got Darby in a whole bunch of trouble to the point where Darby was actually blacklisted from clubs for a while. Later when we were doing *Rock 'n' Roll High School*, Darby, who was also an extra at the Roxy, was crying on my shoulder about the whole ordeal. But then the Germs' fans beat up the Red Army in retaliation. I suppose any publicity was good publicity, right?

Controversy and bad PR always followed Spider. Once I was at this guy's house, and I told him I had to leave to go do the hair for the Red Army. And this dude worked with the police in some way, so he said, "Hold up. Just wait a minute. What do you *mean*, the Red Army? We have instructions to arrest them on sight. Aren't they Communists? Aren't they political?" That's what he thought, that this was some rebel cult or sect that was backing Communism, and that I was tied up in some sort of political revolt.

I said, "Jesus Christ, are you guys out of your mind? They're not political. They're a singing group!" That was hilarious to me.

I was attracting a lot of men during this time, more than I ever had been before, but sometimes I missed a great opportunity. Once when

I was staying at my mother's and all I was doing was sitting around, mindlessly watching television, on all the talk shows and shows about pumping iron was this guy named Arnold Schwarzenegger, who had just done *Stay Hungry*. As it turned out, Arnold lived down the block, and one day when was I walking down to the deli with Lucky, there he was on the street in all his bronzed, brawny glory. I recognized him, so I said, "Oh, hi, how are you? I see you on television a lot." Not my best opening line, but it worked.

Without missing a beat, Arnold picked me up by my belt loops and effortlessly lifted me off the ground, like I was one of his barbells, and he purred, "Why don't you come over to my house? Drop the kid off. Here's my address." I was up for it. So I left Lucky with my mom and headed over to his place.

Arnold was in his downstairs living room with Lou Ferrigno and some other guys from Gold's Gym. For some reason, I was under the stupid impression that all muscle men were gay—I don't know why I would even think that—so I was oblivious to Arnold's true intentions. He and I smoked some pot while he told me about everything he was going to do in his career. He already had his life and plans for world domination all mapped out, even the part about going into politics someday. I just sat there gawking at him. He was gorgeous, albeit much smaller-looking than he seemed on the television when he was flexing and posing, and he was interesting and really made me laugh.

And then, all of a sudden, he pinned me up against the wall and announced, "I want to know what it is to go to bed with you."

I said, "You'll never find out." I thought he was joking because I still thought he was gay. But he also scared me. He was too much for me. He put his arms down and released me, and that was it. Later I regretted turning him down and changed my mind, just like I'd had second thoughts with Al Green. I tried to call Arnold, and I even went over to see him one night, but his mother was there, visiting from

Austria. So that was the end of that. Maybe I should have written him a sexy letter.

I can live with that missed chance, but I will probably never forgive myself for not being more assertive with Bob Dylan. To say I had a crush on Bob Dylan would be the understatement of the millennium. He was my idol, my icon, my everything. The first time I played *The Freewheelin' Bob Dylan*, my whole world changed, and I had been searching for him ever since. One time when I was in Woodstock visiting Miss Christine and her then-boyfriend Todd Rundgren, I'd heard Dylan was in town and I was looking for him then, but we didn't cross paths.

But on one particular magical day around 1978, I could sense Dylan's presence on the street. I kept saying, "I feel Bob Dylan, I feel Bob Dylan." However, I didn't expect to run into him. He was not supposed to come out in broad daylight, I thought. You just don't expect to see Bob Dylan walk out of some building while you're on your lunch break.

I was working for an antique shop in Santa Monica, and Bob was doing the *Street-Legal* album nearby at Rundown Studios. That's where I finally met him. I was just hanging, and there he was. He was really adorable then, with blond hair. He was about to drive away, so I rushed up to his car and ordered, "Roll your window down." Much to my surprise, he actually complied. What were the chances of that happening? He could have sped off in a panic, and I wouldn't have blamed him. I said, "Don't be paranoid."

Bob said, cool as a cucumber, "I'm not."

I didn't bring up who I was. If I had, I think Bob would have flipped out because he was a GTOs fan. I'd always been convinced that his look from the Rolling Thunder Revue was GTOs-inspired, with all the panda eyeliner. I was *so* stupid not to mention it. Instead, I just talked a bunch of shit. I just babbled. I wanted to tell him, "You wrote my life." I longed to tell him that so many of his songs made me go places; I could actually see the films of it in my mind. But instead I went on and on about some dancers that I thought should have been in his actual film, the critically panned *Renaldo and Clara*. He asked me, "Have you even seen *Renaldo and Clara*?" I sheepishly admitted that no, I had not. He said, "Well, listen, do me a favor. Go see it, and afterward I want you to come back and talk to me about what you thought of it." And then he drove away. It was probably the most starstruck I have ever been.

I could have easily taken Dylan up on his invitation. I could have invited him to Johnny Otis's church, because he probably would have been there in a minute. I just never had the nerve to do it. I don't have many regrets in life, but that is the major one. But maybe I just wasn't supposed to get that close. Maybe I was supposed to worship Bob from afar. There's one person in the world that could intimidate me, and it was Bob Dylan. Still, I would really love to find him and have that follow-up conversation someday.

I probably should have just dated Dylan's bodyguard. He had a big crush on me at the time, and I didn't want to hurt his feelings, which was one of the reasons I never tried to pursue Bob. He was this big, fabulous Black man who loved the Soul Stirrers and Sam Cooke, and he'd let me into Dylan's Santa Monica rehearsal hall and we'd listen to soul music together. Then one time he took me out on a date but I had him drive me downtown to look for drugs, and I just fucked everything up.

I reinvented myself in more ways than one in the late seventies. Along with the punk thing and the hairdressing, I had a side gig in hip-hop, managing a pop-locking dance duo called the Boogie Masters. I was dressing sort of like a break-dancer by then. The Gypsy clothes were gone (I still had the eye makeup, of course), and in their place were studded belts wrapped around my legs and a platinum hairdo that I bleached out myself. I looked like Billy Idol at the time, but my style wasn't inspired by Billy; I inspired myself.

Anyway, these Boogie Masters cats, Robert and Darrell, were kind of like Bob Dylan characters. The syncopation of those two was thrilling to behold. I found them on Venice Beach. I'd go down with my son to watch them on the boardwalk, and I was freaked out by their moves. They were a big part of my life for a while. I even put Lucky onstage with them; he couldn't really pop, but he could dance, and I could tell he was at home onstage.

So, I decided I'd be the Boogie Masters' manager. I booked them at this fancy Beverly Hills event, and my friend Patti D'Arbanville, the actress, freaked out over them. She thought they were actually incredible. After that I took them to audition for Danny Fields, the guy who'd managed the Stooges and Ramones, but he told me, "They're really incredible, but there's no work for them. Nobody uses these people. There's nothing we can do with them." Years later, the Boogie Masters would have been totally accepted. They were doing what Michael Jackson did, what Usher does, what Chris Brown does. The moves have been passed down. But I tried and tried for about eight months because I really believed in them. The biggest gig I got them was a bar mitzvah. They were paid about $500 for that.

Many, many years later, I was catching the subway train at the Hollywood and Highland station, and I saw these pop-locking street performers, all dressed in metallic gold—gold suit, gold sequins, gold face paint. I did a double-take and said to myself, "That can't be. These can't be my Venice people!" And then one of them said to me, "Oh, hey, Mercy." It was Darrell, still popping, still getting funky.

I had an affair with one of the Boogie Masters, but he was *way* too young. I didn't know he was fifteen, okay? He told me he was eighteen. But drugs still ruled my life more than sex, as had always been the case. Heroin was really popular in the punk scene, also because it was cut with fentanyl, which was fifty to a hundred times stronger than morphine. Later I heard that some physician or dentist had brought fentanyl to San Diego and was adding it to the mix, and that's what was happening. It took one matchhead in that heroin to kill you. A lot of people were dying. People died after one hit, the first time they ever did it. I would sit with people at the table at the Starwood, and they'd suddenly lapse into a coma right in the middle of a conversation. So I called up the *LA Weekly* and said, "Look, there's something very fucked up going on, and you guys need to do some kind of exposé, because this is killing people." In the next *Weekly* that came out, there was a story about this on the front page.

Speed was more my thing. In my GTOs day, I was always trying to score speed, and it was nearly impossible—but when I came back into the punk scene, I conveniently discovered that the drug of choice was a type of speed called Preludin. The speed was inside the pill, so you had to crack it open to get the little bit of speed that was in there and melt it and cook it. But then I met an older speed freak—Marty, about age fifty—in my Hollywood apartment building. He would never do methamphetamine from the street. He got pure pharmaceutical pills, Desoxyn, and would soak them.

One day I was at Marty's place and he was sick so he couldn't do any speed, so I went in his bathroom, and in the cabinet was this yellow liquid where he would soak these pills for days. It very, very yellow, and very, very strong. Without saying anything to him—it was only me and him in the apartment—I got a syringe, siphoned his dope out of the bottle, and started to fix. And then, I started to rush— and you don't usually do that on amphetamines, so it must've been strong. I thought to myself, "Should I finish this shot or not? This is kind of crazy. Why am I rushing?" But of course I finished the shot, and then when I sat down in a chair, everywhere around me I started seeing tracers and I knew something was very wrong.

I couldn't look anywhere because everything I saw was multiplied, 100 of everything. I'd seen tracers before, of course, but nothing like this. I couldn't even close my eyes without seeing tracers. Marty had like fifty arms, sixty eyeballs. It was a massive hallucination, like something out *Fear and Loathing in Las Vegas*. I knew I was very close to like overdosing on what I had just taken. "Shit, I might blow my brains out with this shot. I think this is the end of the road here," I thought grimly.

I was pretty terrified at that point, so I confessed to Marty what I had done. He screamed, "What have you done? That's *pure Desoxyn!*" I tried to keep calm. I was thinking, "I'm either going to die, or things are going to get better. I don't know which one it's going to be. If I go, I go." But eventually my heart started beating more slowly and the tracers started to subside. So I made it through that. But I know for a fact I was very close to having a brain hemorrhage, and I've always believed that this particular overdose did a lot of damage. That was probably the time I was closest to death. But I got myself together and still went to the Starwood that night anyway, as I had planned.

Death was always a very real possibility in the punk world. I was at the Whisky the night that Exene Cervenka's sister Mirielle was killed in a hit-and-run accident on the way to an X gig. I was with the Gears when their manager ran up to us, stage-whispering, "How are we going to tell Exene? How are we going to tell her?" It was all so shocking. But X still went onstage. I figured Exene would not be able to even deal with it, but they performed the *best* set. It was really fucking weird to me, very eerie and very trippy. Mirielle had just done a movie with her husband, *Ecstatic Stigmatic*, and in one scene she was lying in a coffin with blood seeping from her hands, like she had stigmata. I saw the film after the tragedy, and I was sitting there watching this going, "Oh, my God, they're touching on something. They played with fire."

Mirielle was dead in real life, and she was dead in this movie. I stumbled into the lobby in a daze, and Mirielle's husband, Gordon Stevenson, was out there, pacing. I told him, "Maybe you shouldn't have filmed that. Maybe you were not supposed to do that."

He said, "Maybe you're right." That was very heavy. Gordon died of AIDS just a couple years after that.

I actually almost got killed in my first Hollywood apartment, the same night that Pure Hell played and Steve Olson gave me a ride home. I'd been doing some speed, and I felt like somebody was watching me. But maybe I was just being paranoid, I thought. When I got home, I was sitting there on my couch and there was a knock at the door. I stupidly said, "I don't know if I locked the door or not. Who is it?" And I thought the guy said, "A menace." I don't know if he said that, but that's what it sounded like.

The menacing man came walking in through the door, straight at me, and tried to push me out my window. I picked up an ashtray and threw it at him and ran out of the apartment—left my purse with all my cash, and just started running. My building had heavy steel fire doors in between corridors, and I kept running, slamming each door hard behind me, running and running as fast as I could. I was knocking on people's doors, screaming for help, but all my asshole neighbors did was push me out. Finally a mother and a child let me in their place. I howled, "This guy just attacked me!" So the kid grabbed a baseball bat. It seemed the coast was clear, so I thanked the mother and told her I would be fine. But as soon as I left, the menace reappeared in the hallway. The guy had been waiting for me under the stairs. So I ran back to the mother and son's apartment, and I spent the night there.

The next day I saw the man—it was one of the building's maintenance guys. I reported the incident to my landlady while the mother was there with me. I thought the mother was going to back me up, but she bizarrely didn't; maybe she was too afraid this guy

Mercy Fontenot and Lyndsey Parker

would come after her next. Instead, she said, "I didn't see anybody." I thought, "What the fuck's going on here?" It was crazy. So I moved out right away. I didn't know what this lunatic wanted from me—he already had my money—and I didn't want to find out. That was one of the freakiest, most frightening things that ever happened to me.

Hollywood back then was a scary place. People were getting killed left and right. I would come home and guns were pulled on me. Of course these situations scared the hell out of me. But there were plenty of other situations where I wasn't scared. I probably should have been scared, but I could deal with it. But that situation was one I couldn't deal with because I didn't know the outcome or reason. The other ones I could handle because I knew why.

Unfortunately, trouble followed me to my next Hollywood apartment. I was at the Troubadour one night and I ran into a young girl from my Hollywood hair school. A friend said to me, "Beware of what you're getting into," but I didn't pay any attention to him, and when the club closed and the girl didn't want to go back to her parents' house so late, I offered to let her crash at my place. I took her back to my apartment, and the walls were all decorated with photos of the Rockats modeling my hairdos, my signature stiff quiffs. I told the girl, "We've got to call your mother. You can't just stay out all night and worry her." So I phoned her mom and said, "Your daughter's over at my house." And the mom said, "Okay, we'll pick her up tomorrow." The mother and her boyfriend came by the next day, and I asked if they could give me a ride to visit my mom in Santa Monica, where I had plans to meet up with Lucky.

So they sat me in the backseat with the girl, and the girl said, "Can't you drop Mercy off first, Mom?"—which would, of course, have made more sense. But they said, "No, we're going to drop you off first." That should have been a red flag, but I shrugged it off. The mother and the girl went in their house for a minute, and when the mother came out by herself and got back in the car, she was brandishing a knife. She told me, "We're going to kill you. We saw all those pictures of those dyke girls on your walls. You lesbian bitch!" This madwoman had mistaken the pinups of the Rockats pretty-boys for photos of chicks. The boyfriend stepped on the gas, and I thought, "Oh, shit, I'm in big trouble now."

We pulled up onto a side street and the boyfriend struck me hard, right across the face. They kept saying, "We're going to kill you, we're going to kill you!" I assumed they were crazy homophobes and they thought I was some older lesbian predator who had molested their daughter, or had tried to. I was sure they were going to hack me to pieces—until they saw a security guard in the alley, so they called it off. The boyfriend hit me as hard as he fucking could one more time, then pushed me out of the car and sped off—but not before he said, "If you go back to that school, we will kill you. We know where you live."

Later I called my beauty school teacher, who adored me, in hysterics, and I told him what happened. "These people are going to murder me!" I sobbed.

He said, "Obviously it is not safe for you to return to class. So I'm going to pass you for state board. I'll give you your hours and say you passed." But then I still had to take the state board test, and I didn't know shit. I only knew how to do the punk stuff. So I failed the test, and I never got my cosmetology license.

I never would have been able to graduate beauty school. I could never get the real basics down. I could not do their normal things. I couldn't finger-wave or do permanents; I only knew how to do stuff that I made up. I only had my own style going on. But I didn't really want to be a hairdresser as a profession anyway. Who wants to stand on their feet eight hours a day and do that? Doing hair was fun for a while, but I didn't want to do it forever. I just wanted to be part of the scene. I only wanted to make a splash and then get out. Like I always do.

11

Ḧard Working Woman

IT WAS NEVER A goal for me to be famous. I wanted to be infamous.

If you look at my astrological chart, most of my planets are in the house of public, the eleventh house, the house of Aquarius—which would therefore make me, if you believe in astrology, a public figure. So I was destined to live my life publicly. That doesn't mean that I was destined to make a bunch of money, however.

People have asked me why I didn't get more into music, why I didn't start another band after the GTOs broke up or pursue some sort of solo career. A lot of fans have told me my songs were the two best tracks on the GTOs album. I'm proud of those songs, but I knew I was no musician. I was more interested in being a networker than doing my own music. I felt it was my calling to hook people together and evangelize other artists.

Besides, I couldn't see myself having to play the same song over and over again.

Looking back, I realize I should have given music a real try. How dumb was I? I had everything at my disposal to launch my own musical career. I had the most talented people you can imagine, the most talented people in the world, right in front of me. I was literally surrounded by *The Johnny Otis Show*. And I let it pass me by. I could have made an album in Hawk Sound with a cast of all-star musicians that'd practically make Jeff Beck and Rod Stewart look like amateurs by comparison. At the very least, I could have joined Johnny Otis's choir and learned how to properly sing, but I didn't even do that. To me, Shuggie was the artist, so I was a good little wifey and stayed in my lane.

The only thing I ever tried to sing on, besides the GTOs album, was the Flying Burrito Brothers' "Hippie Boy." Pamela and I were called in to do that, but we were *supposed* to be out of tune—which, if you've ever listened to the GTOs' music, you know wasn't too hard for us to do. It was a joke. It's not like we were trying to be the *20 Feet From Stardom* girls.

I could've gotten all the voice lessons in the world. Taj Mahal once told me, "I'd really love to teach you how to sing," and I never took him up on it. Another mistake.

Taj and I were close friends in the sixties, during the GTOs days. He wanted to give me vocal lessons, but we never got it together to do that; maybe if we had, I would have ended up singing on more of the GTOs album, or pursued some sort of solo music. I didn't see very much of Taj for a long time, but years later I went to a blues festival where he was the headliner, so I sent him a message that I was backstage. After the show, he found me and I went back to the hotel with him. But it was just a one-night affair. It just fell into place. And then he sent me a postcard from Paris to my mother's apartment that simply read "I love you very much." I tried to phone him after that but couldn't reach him, so I figured, "Well, I guess that's my Taj Mahal story." I never saw him again. We obviously weren't meant to be partners, professionally or personally.

My one other time, besides that jokey Burritos session, when I attempted to contribute to another artist's record was when

Christine was living with Todd Rundgren in New York State. Todd was engineering the Band's *Stage Fright* album, so I hitchhiked there to hang out. Rick Danko was there, and I would've actually loved to go to bed with him, but I didn't go after him at all. It didn't even dawn on me to try. That's when the weight issue comes in, maybe. Sometimes I didn't even think to go after the people I wanted because of my weight. I was probably scared of being turned down, but some of my crushes might have said yes. We'll never know. Anyway, I was trying to feed Rick some lyrics for "Stage Fright," but he wasn't having it and he didn't use any of them. Still, that was a blast.

I figured there were other ways for me to get onstage and be a performer or artist. For instance, not long after I arrived in LA, I decided to be a nude dancer. Back in the late sixties and early seventies, if a gal needed work and she didn't want to be a hooker, she became a stripper. My friend arranged for me to audition for a strip show because she said it was good, easy money, and we went up to this house in the hills. I was ordered to disrobe, like I was at the doctor's office. Total nudity was required—no pasties, no G-strings, no boa feathers. The other auditioners and I did our thing, like we were trying out for an X-rated version of *American Idol* in front of this panel behind a table. And then I heard one of the men who was judging us say to his boss. "Well, one girl can dance, one is beautiful, and the other one is a no." I was the first one.

After passing that test, they put me on a plane to some weird town somewhere up north, in the middle of nowhere, and I danced there. I stayed in a motel, but after one night's work, I went home. That was a tacky place, and it all felt so shady. But nothing happened to me, thank God. When I somehow returned to LA—and I literally don't recall how I made it back—I figured it was time to upgrade, so I applied at the world-famous Body Shop on Sunset, as immortalized many years later in Mötley Crüe's "Girls, Girls, Girls."

Every night at the Body Shop I'd come out, shimmy to some soul music, and split. None of the patrons were allowed to talk to me or touch me. It was all very cool, actually. But that was another early job that didn't last long because I became more seriously involved with Shuggie, and he obviously would not have stood for it. I remember being in the phone booth in front of the Body Shop and calling Shuggie's house, and I got Phyllis on the line. She told me Shuggie was flying back from London that day, so I convinced a friend to drive me to LAX, surprised him when he got off the plane, and went home with him and never went back to nude dancing. But I enjoyed it; it was a pretty sweet, cushy gig.

Another job involving nudity didn't go so well for me.

I first met Alice Cooper through Christine, who, like Pamela, Cynderella, and myself, had this radar for finding the next big thing. Christine was really gaga for Alice, who was her boyfriend for a while. She took me to a rehearsal, but I didn't think that much of him at first—he wasn't "Alice" yet, he was just Vince Furnier. But Christine saw something special in him, tipped him off to Frank Zappa, and the Alice Cooper Band signed to Frank's label, Straight Records. I truly believe Christine helped Vince transform into Alice. And all of us GTOs influenced his image. We'd take Vince to the thrift shops and dress him up, and I know my Theda Bara makeup partially inspired his own spooky face paint. Maybe that was why I was never physically attracted to Alice, even though I adored him—he was too much like me. I usually don't get turned on by somebody who's my twin.

Anyway, by 1971 Alice had signed to Warner Bros., and Warner was celebrating with a fancy "Coming Out" party at the Ambassador Hotel on July 14. Alice got in touch and asked me if I would jump out of this seven-foot-tall cake that said "Happy Bastille Day" on it. Warner hired me along with the Cockettes, who were the waitresses. One Cockette, dressed as a cigarette girl with a tray hanging from their neck, was walking around chanting, "Cigars, cigarettes, Vaseline!" I really wanted to get high that night because I wanted to get high every night, so I ducked into the pantry and smoked some angel dust, as one does.

I was supposed to pop out of the cake nude, but right before my big unveiling, somebody mentioned to me, "You know, this hotel is where Bobby Kennedy was killed." I just *flipped out*. And then they stuffed me in the cake.

I kept my Moroccan robe on at the last minute, refusing to strip down. By the time the cake got wheeled out, I was freaking out so hard that I took pieces of the cake and started throwing them into the crowd. This was a new sort of sugar high. "What the fuck am I doing here?" I howled, as I let the frosting fly.

I'm sure that question was on everyone's mind and lips. I hit Rod McKuen right in the face, which I know because he wrote a letter about it that got published in the newspaper: "I want to thank Mercy for the cake in the face. Love, Rod McKuen." Richard Chamberlain and members of the Beach Boys were in attendance too, and I'm sure they also got frosted.

Incidentally, Alice Cooper wasn't the only shock-rocker who derived cosmetic inspiration from the GTOs. I always thought Paul Stanley from KISS got his painted star from Miss Sandra, because if you look at the photos from our album cover, she has a black star painted on her pregnant belly and black stars around her eyes. I don't think that was a coincidence. Gene Simmons actually once told me to my face, "You *know* where I got my look, Mercy. You *know* where we got our makeup." Then he added, "But you need to get off drugs." Of course, I did not heed Gene's advice.

After I got fired from the GTOs, I decided my next career reinvention would be as some sort of femme fatale star of stage and screen. I even had a professional acting headshot taken of me wearing a platinum wig and movie-star cat-eye makeup. That's my favorite photo of myself; I'm very skinny in that picture. I had been obsessed with the magic of Hollywood moviemaking since I was a little girl. Warren Low, an esteemed film editor who worked on Elvis Presley movies like *Blue Hawaii, G.I. Joe*, and *King Creole* as well as *The Bad Seed* and *True Grit*, was my uncle by marriage—my father's sister had married Warren—and I was more impressed by him than by any other relative. As a kid, I would come down to LA to visit Warren almost every Christmas, and he had Elvis postcards for Christmas cards. Hanging out at his house instilled in me a lifelong love of cinema.

Rebel Without a Cause, Gypsy, Nashville, Citizen Kane, and *Some Came Running* with Frank Sinatra, Dean Martin, and Shirley MacLaine—these are some of my favorite films. But my all-time favorite has always been *West Side Story*. Throughout my life, I watched it over and over and memorized that entire damn thing. And I was smitten with the dreamy Russ Tamblyn, who played Riff, leader of the Jets. So when I was living in LA, I was determined to go visit him. Cynderella figured out that he lived in Topanga Canyon, and we went right up and knocked on his door. For some reason, he let us in, and we smoked some pot with him. I was sitting in his living room, stoned, thinking, "Oh, my God, I can't even comprehend this." But I wasn't after Russ in a sexual way; I just wanted to be in the presence of greatness. Later, one night in Laurel Canyon, Russ visited me out of nowhere. He sat down in his little teeny chair, like a child's chair, and he promptly broke it. I still don't know why he came to see me, but he did and it was nice. We just talked.

I'd already done the Hendrix movie *Rainbow Bridge*, of course, but then again, I was playing myself in that. I was always "myself"— that was the role I was born to play, I guess. But *Rainbow Bridge* wasn't my first time gracing the silver screen. In 1968, shortly after

I arrived in Los Angeles, my gal pal Ricky Klampert and I landed bit parts in Otto Preminger's *Skidoo*, a movie basically about Jackie Gleason on acid. Some of *Skidoo*'s other stars were Frankie Avalon, John Phillip Law, Peter Lawford, Burgess Meredith, George Raft, Cesar Romero, Mickey Rooney, Carol Channing, and Groucho Marx. It was just about the most sixties thing ever. I had this amazing, feather-trimmed lavender robe that had supposedly belonged to Jean Harlow—one of my all-time favorite pieces of clothing; a gay guy that lived under a Laurel Canyon store gave it to me—and I layered it on top of a colorful striped dress, and Ricky and I marched down to try out for the picture. Otto took one look at us and declared, "You're hired! You're in!" I wish I still had that robe.

We were up on some mountain in this beautiful house with Carol Channing, believe it or not. She was fucking fabulous. Ricky and I had great fun getting high on pot with John Phillip Law, and I saw Jackie Gleason taking LSD, or at least pretending to. (I believe he really did—method acting, you know.) But my time on the set was short-lived; I guess I just wasn't ready for my close-up. I was supposed to shoot a second scene running from a courthouse, but I had stupidly changed my outfit, being as clothes-obsessed as I was. Otto went nuts, yelling, "Get out of there! Get her *out*!" I'd ruined the whole continuity of the film. I was dismissed from the production.

My acting career never got off the ground, but much later, in my punk days, I starred in an unreleased movie with El Duce from the Mentors called *The Saint Comes to Hollywood*. The Mentors were very misogynist; they described their music as "rape rock." El Duce scared the daylights out of me. There's an urban legend out there that he was hired by Courtney Love to kill Kurt Cobain, and while I don't believe that, he seemed like the type you'd hire for that sort of thing—brutal and nasty. He grossed me out. But after making a movie with him, I realized he was one of the sweetest people on the planet.

This all came about when I was walking down Sunset Boulevard and spotted El Duce shooting this low-low-budget exploitation flick. I didn't know El Duce, but I certainly knew his reputation. I still have no idea what got into me—I was probably high on something—but I walked right up to the director and said, "I would like to be in this movie." Much to my surprise, the director said, "Okay, you can play El Duce's wife." True Hollywood story! If only all auditions were that easy.

The director and El Duce and I went to local legendary photographer Gary Leonard's house to shoot a sequence in which I was singing some blues number—a Muddy Waters song, I believe. I guess that counts as another one of my career attempts at making music. Then we shot a scene on a truck with El Duce beating the fuck out of me, or pretending to. The truck was parked right in front of my old apartment where I'd been attacked and nearly pushed out the window, and as El Duce was fake-beating me, my attacker, the menacing maintenance man, walked on by. That was very weird. But I tried to stay in character and be a professional.

There was another scene with me smoking crack, and I really *was* smoking crack. Like I said, method acting! Talk about commitment to the role, right? In another scene, I was in bed with these underage kids from a local teen punk band, pretending to be a prostitute. An older brother got in the bed and threw them out, then El Duce became an angel and everybody got saved. I suppose now it's pretty obvious why this movie never came out. And I never did get paid. But I did get the director addicted to crack. The last time I saw him, he was pushing a shopping cart and selling miniature palm trees on the street.

Another unreleased punk movie, the Gears' *The Dye Job*, was about me. This documentarian who was shooting stuff about the Gears told them, "Your hairdresser is *fascinating*. Let's do a movie

Mercy Fontenot *and* Lyndsey Parker

with her!" It was all about me doing Spike's hair. I was supposed to attend the premiere, but I did too much speed, so I didn't even show up at my own event. It's a terrible, cringeworthy film, to be honest; I loathed it when I finally watched it, some thirty years later. It's pretty much just a home movie, and I come across as the most obnoxious, over-amphetamined person you have ever seen. I should have won all the Golden Raspberries. *The Dye Job* is impossible to find now, thank God, but parts of it show up in the far superior Gears documentary *Don't Be Afraid to Pogo*.

In the late eighties, I was in Oliver Stone's *The Doors* movie, in a party scene. I heard that they were shooting and went down there out of curiosity, and this casting agent saw me and said, "Oh, you've *got* to meet Oliver. He simply must meet you, because you're the original and you're really *it*. I mean, you're *from* that era!" So they put me in as an extra, but then they left my footage on the cutting-room floor. I think I was too flashy and out-there, because I was so real—too real. Also, I was nearly forty years old and didn't fit in with all those young, nubile extras. But it was a trippy experience. I almost felt like I was back in time. Val Kilmer was so beautiful, and he did such a stellar job that it was like Jim Morrison had come back from the dead.

One other attempt I made at getting fewer than twenty feet from stardom was when I auditioned for the roller derby. I was in hair school on Hollywood Boulevard at the time, and some of the other hairdressers were on the Thunderbirds team. I'd spent much of my childhood being dropped off at the local roller rink while my parents were off gambling at the races, so I'd learned how to speed skate and I figured I'd be a roller derby natural. And at that time, believe it or not, Johnny and Shuggie Otis were doing the in-between roller derby music show as well as the official theme music for the Thunderbirds—though I swear that's not why I was interested. I just wanted to audition to see if I could do it.

So I went over to the Thunderbirds' practice rink downtown, and I started skating like crazy, showing off and trying to impress everyone. These groovy soul records were playing, motivating me, so I kept picking up speed, and then when Wilson Pickett came on, I started *really* gunning it. I went full blast. I was zipping along when suddenly all the lights went out and I couldn't see anything. I threw my arms up and hit the wall, crashed to the floor, and my shoulder blade popped way out of its alignment. I started shrieking in agony, and this jerk rolled up to me and said, "Don't be such a sissy!"

I yelled back, "Look at my collar bone, asshole. It's sticking out! Please, just call an ambulance." Over at the hospital I tried for hours to get a shot of something to ease the pain, but there was some lady that had been run over by a lawnmower and she was getting all the medics' attention. I kept howling, "I need a shot, I need a shot! I really hurt!" Finally I got it, and they jammed my shoulder back in place and sent me on my way.

Later I was dropping Lucky off at the Otis house and wearing a sling, and Johnny asked me, "What on earth is wrong with your arm?"

I said, "I broke it trying out for roller derby."

He barked, "What in the world are you doing, at age twenty-seven, trying out for the roller derby? Let me call this guy over there. We happen to do the theme song and we're their entertainment; I've got connections." Johnny was really good at getting money. He once sued the Magic Mountain theme park because the stage collapsed there. He was that kind of guy.

Johnny got on the phone and said all seriously, "Hey, I got my ex-daughter-in-law here, and..." The man on the end of the line panicked before Johnny had even finished uttering his sentence.

"Is that where she is? We've been wondering where she went. Who is that lady? What happened? We're freaking out!" the roller derby dude exclaimed.

Mercy Fontenot *and* Lyndsey Parker

Johnny said, "She's right here. She's okay, for the most part, but she'd like some money."

The guy asked, "Well, how much does she want?"

I had no idea this injury would ruin whatever hairdressing career I had, or might ever want to have. I couldn't pick up my scissors. I couldn't do anything. I was hurt, and I probably still am hurt. I could have sued for thousands of dollars. I mean, the Thunderbirds folks were genuinely scared, quaking in their boots—or in their skates. But like an idiot, I said, "I'll take $300 under the table." The next day, $300 cash in an unmarked envelope was delivered to my door, and that was the end of that. Oh, well.

12

Ḫome Is Where the Ḫatred Is

I ADORE MY SON, Lucky, with all my heart. If I did one thing right in my life, this crazy life of mine, it was having him. But sometimes I think maybe I just wasn't meant to be a mother.

Motherhood was never part of the original Shuggie dream I'd had. When I was pregnant, I felt no joy. I felt nothing. I'm not sure why. It may have been because when I got knocked up, I quit all drugs right away, and that could have jolted me into a depression. Maybe I had pre-partum depression. I am positive I had the postpartum kind. That's probably why I went right back on the drugs.

When Lucky came out, however, I immediately bonded with him and fell head over heels for him. He became my whole world for a while; Shuggie became a very distant second. But then I started getting so strung out on drugs that everything became secondary to my addictions. Right there is your evidence that motherhood might not have been my calling.

My mother was actually thrilled when I left Shuggie and turned up with Lucky on her doorstep. She hadn't wanted me to marry Shuggie in the first place—"He's one of the dumbest people I've ever met," she used to say—and I think she was lonely after my dad died. She adored Lucky and was delighted to have this new playmate with her, so before you know it, I was the third wheel. So, I'd leave my mom and son alone and go off to do my punk thing in Hollywood.

My mom and I lived together on and off for ten years, and we became closer than we ever had before. Looking back, I realize she was a big reason why I walked out on Shuggie. Yes, the Teri love triangle was an obvious factor, but my mother had nobody but me and Lucky at this point, and I felt a duty to spend time with her. I hadn't been with her much when I was young and had never really had a childhood. I wanted to do all that before she left this planet.

Unfortunately, I got more and more addicted to drugs, right in front of my mom. Eventually, Lucky ended up living most of the time with the Otises.

This is how that happened: I had tried to put him in public school, and his birthday was December 3 and it turned out December 2 was the cutoff date for his local kindergarten, so he was going to have to stay back a grade. I protested, "But my kid's a genius! My kid is amazing! He can recite the alphabet backward!" But the school board refused to make any exceptions to this rule. I was beside myself. I called Johnny Otis from a pay phone on Hollywood Boulevard, bawling hysterically.

He said, "What are you crying about? What the hell is wrong with your mind?"

I just kept sobbing and sobbing, and at one point I exclaimed, "You have to take care of my son! I can't do it!"

Then he said, "Okay, okay, I'm coming to get Lucky. Stay there." Apparently Johnny had already written a letter to my mother that read, "Don't worry about Lucky. I will take care of him. Kids should not have kids." That's how he felt about me and Shuggie. He wasn't wrong.

Lucky has felt abandoned ever since, and I understand why. I understand now what Christmases must have felt like to him. Even though he stayed with me or my mother most weekends, and he lived with me off and on, as I got more into drugs, I would disappear. I may have known where Lucky was, but *he* didn't know where *I* was. And then I would pop up suddenly and follow him around. I realize now that this completely messed with his developing mind.

But at the time, I honestly believed I was being a great mom and doing what was best for him. My thought was always, "Well, maybe Lucky was abandoned, but look *where* he got abandoned!" The benefits of living in the Otis house, I rationalized, balanced out any negative effects of the abandonment. After all, Lucky was surrounded by *The Johnny Otis Show* and this rich musical lifestyle, and of course that was the best thing in the world for him, right? It would be his twenty-four-seven, immersive musical bootcamp, his school-of-hard-rocks education.

Obviously, Lucky didn't have a very stable home life, but he had a great *music* life. Everything that he got exposed to growing up with Shuggie and Johnny, and just having that in his bloodline, made him insanely talented. His musical talent still blows me away today and fills me to bursting with pride. Johnny noticed Lucky's genius first. Johnny would call me up and say, "Your son has such a great voice," or, "Your son's really gifted." Maybe Johnny wanted Lucky to be the next Shuggie since the first Shuggie never really obeyed him. Johnny gave Lucky a bass guitar; I went and hocked it for some crack, and Johnny got really mad, but he just bought a new one. And that's when Lucky started playing with Johnny.

But Shuggie wasn't in Lucky's life much either, especially after he and Teri had their son, Eric. Shuggie favored Eric over Lucky; I think he *had* to, because Teri ran his world. It was a terrible position for Lucky to be in, abandoned by both his mom and dad. Additionally,

Teri didn't want me anywhere near her husband, so Lucky living in the Otis house caused many problems in that regard as well. There was always a lot of competitiveness in the Otis family—Johnny versus Shuggie, Shuggie versus Lucky, Lucky versus Eric. Both Eric and Lucky would play and tour with Shuggie over the years, but Eric was always more straitlaced and not as flamboyant as my son, more the type to just stand in the back and not steal the spotlight from his dad, so Shuggie tended to work more with Eric.

Lucky loved music, but he also hated it, because he saw it as something competing for his mother's attention, something taking his mom away from him. For instance, I once took him to the Cathay de Grande when he was little, and he still complains about that incident today. He tells this tragic tale about how I left him upstairs with the bartender. He remains traumatized by that. But oddly, that's not at all how *I* remember it; I remember taking him to see Devo and everyone fawning over him, with the band even asking him to go onstage, and I remember being so proud of him. I took Lucky out with me a lot because he was my son and I was trying to introduce him to cool music and interesting people early on. My intentions were good. I wanted him to be part of my world, of the music world. But he was way too young to appreciate it, and I should have realized that.

Lucky was furious with me growing up, and he's still furious, all the time. We love each other madly, and there's still a united front there; we're each other's people. But there's also this strange animosity between us because he's very hard-headed and so am I. Sometimes he'll randomly show up on my doorstep to surprise me with an invitation to dinner, but then other times he randomly calls me to yell stuff like, "You're a crackhead. You left me. You sold my guitar; you sold my records!" Every evil thing that I ever did when I was using, he rattles off the list.

I always tell him, "I'm sorry. I'm *really* sorry. Can't you just forget? Or *forgive*?" Eventually I hang up on him because I can't handle him throwing everything back in my face. When he flashes back, I try to escape it, because I don't want to feel any guilt. It hurts too much because I know he is right, and I know there is nothing short of getting in a time machine to undo what I did in the past.

At the time of this writing, Lucky and I are not talking. I don't even know where he's living. I don't know if we will ever repair our relationship. I so desperately want to make up for all that wasted time, but I know I don't have that much time left now. Sometimes when Lucky would visit me right around the time I got sober for good, in the late nineties, all I could think of was the past that I'd tried to block out for so long. My room always seemed so empty after he'd leave; it held his essence, but also such an emptiness, and my eyes would flood with tears. I'd think of all those years I could have spent with him, or *should* have spent with him, and I'd cry like a baby every time. I sometimes deeply regret that I didn't stay married and try to fix the Shuggie situation so that Lucky could have a happy home, some semblance of a normal boyhood. But I try not to live on the regrets. I just can't. Lucky, however, thrives on them.

But anyway, despite all the turmoil surrounding Lucky's childhood in the seventies and eighties, I always knew my son was safe, somewhere being cared for. I made sure of that, whether it was with my mom part-time or over at the Otis house. But eventually my mother couldn't care for Lucky anymore because she was dying of breast cancer. The cancer had metastasized and was eating her chest out, and she refused to do anything about it.

I stopped taking all drugs when my mother told me she was dying. I know that sounds like a good thing, but trust me, it was not. The shock of going cold turkey, combined with my mother's illness, sent me downward-spiraling into the darkest depression and deepest sorrow of my life. I think there was some unresolved, residual postpartum depression from Lucky, and on top of that, I'd never really processed the dissolution of my marriage to Shuggie. So even drugs, something I had loved so much, I didn't care about anymore. I couldn't even listen to music. Nothing made any sense to me. Nothing interested me.

My mom went up to my sister's house in Lake County, Northern California, to die. I didn't go up north with her because I was in no condition to take care of myself, let alone my mother. My mother left me in her apartment—the very same apartment where my father had taken his life—and I just could not handle it. I couldn't stand being within those four claustrophobic walls because they contained so many memories. So I would walk the streets for hours and hours. Once I walked around carrying all our old family photos and accidentally left them on a bus stop bench while I was in a fog. I came back, but the photographs were gone, lost forever. I just couldn't get a grip on anything. Pamela would let me come over to her house sometimes so she could keep an eye on me, and she'd helplessly watch as I paced back and forth like a caged animal.

I tried to visit my mom up north, but every time I'd get on an airplane, I'd freak out and beg to be let off, just screaming, "Stop the plane! I don't wanna go, I don't wanna go, I don't wanna go! I've got to get off this airplane!" And in those pre-9/11 days, the stewardesses would allow me to disembark. And then I'd call my mother from an LAX pay phone and tell her, "I was going to come see you."

She'd bark back, "Why didn't you?" But I couldn't bear to see her in her decaying state. In hindsight, I realize I didn't know a thing about coming off drugs—like the proper and safe way to kick— because nobody really talked about that then. So I was probably having some sort of psychotic break.

I didn't fly up north until after my mother was actually gone. My mother died by suicide, technically, though the circumstances were obviously very different from my father's. She simply knew the cancer was killing her, so she hurried up the inevitable on Thanksgiving by feasting on some stockpiled pills. When I got the news, I felt like my foundation had been yanked out from under me. I fell to pieces. It was at this point that I realized I was having a nervous breakdown, so it seemed like a wise idea to go live on my sister Sandra's farm and start my life over. I ended up staying with her for about a year and a half, and we grew close and came to love each other fiercely, like real sisters. As kids, we hadn't been that way, since she was so much older than me and had moved out before I'd gotten to know her.

I'd never really undergone any sort of therapy. My mother had dragged me to a psychiatrist once, right after I got arrested for morphine with Christine. I took some sort of IQ test and scored in the top percentile for "reasoning," believe it or not, and the doctors amusingly told me, "Maybe your *mother* needs therapy instead." Then, I went to Shuggie's shrink once, some guy who had supposedly treated Richard Nixon for amphetamine use, because his family wanted me to go, because Shuggie was crazy. I know that's not very nice to say, but everyone thought Shuggie was insane. Anyway, I had a little meeting with Shuggie's doctor, but it didn't go anywhere. Soon after I arrived in Lake County, however, my worried sister took me to a psychiatrist. He wanted to put me on meds, but I told him, "Hell, no, I'm not going on any psych pills. They're poison." That was probably the only time I said no to drugs.

I'd planned to stay totally sober when I moved north, but as luck, or bad luck, would have it, Kelseyville, where my sister lived, was a speed town, and there was pretty much nothing else to do. It was the pear capital of the world, but apparently it was the speed capital of the world as well. Lake County is right next to Humboldt and used to be a moonshine mecca, so any place that used to be a white lightning facility had been converted into a meth lab. The area was absolutely inundated with meth.

I actually did try to build some sort of legitimate, straight-and-narrow life for myself in Lake County. I moved out of my sister's house and rented my own aluminum trailer right next to the lake where rockabilly star Johnny Burnette had drowned, got a job as a maid at the local inn, and even had Lucky move up north to be with me for a while. But then one of Lucky's teachers was a meth dealer, and she became my connection. Like I said, speed was everywhere in this one-street cockamamie town. And so all my old habits came back, and soon I was doing speed all the time. Between that and the caustic chemical poisoning from all the cleaning products I was being exposed to daily, I was not in great shape.

But the good news is, I got through it. Ironically, I got out of my funk by starting to smoke speed again. It took me four years to come out of my trance, but I finally did. Maybe this was not the best way to self-medicate, but I had to come out of my haze somehow, by any means necessary—it was either that or kill myself too. However, I would *not* recommend speed as a long-term cure-all for depression, kids. Don't try this at home.

13

A House Is Not a Motel

IT WAS BERNARDO SALDANA who got me hooked on crack. When I moved back down to LA after my self-imposed Lake County exile, I stayed with Bernardo, who had apparently become a crack addict while I was gone, so I tried it with him. I didn't particularly care for it. I hardly thought, "Wow, this is the best thing ever!" That attitude would soon change.

I don't resent Bernardo for introducing me to crack. Why should I be mad at him? It would've happened anyway. It was actually hard *not* to smoke crack then, because it was everywhere. Hollywood had been taken over by the 18th Street gang, on every corner. Everybody was smoking crack. Before you knew it, so was I. It was easier to join 'em than to fight 'em, because that's all there was.

There was no high, really. That was the big joke about that drug. I would take a hit of a pipe, and nothing would happen, so I'd do another hit. And then, for some reason, I'd want to hit the pipe again. It was a crazy, chasing-the-dragon kind of trip. I got addicted to it. I wanted it again and again, even though there wasn't anything to really want. It was a big game, a losing game.

Bernardo had fallen on some tough, tragic times since I'd been with him. He'd married Johanna Brighton, one of the loveliest women I'd ever seen, an Amazonian, high-cheekboned, classic beauty who wore bedazzled Nudie Cohn suits and antique thirties garments. She and Bernardo were such a stunning couple. But then she disappeared. The police found her car, with her rhinestone belts and turquoise jewelry in the trunk, but they never found her body. Nobody knows what happened to Johanna, to this day. Johanna's mysterious disappearance absolutely crushed Bernardo. So he turned to crack, and I can't say I blamed him.

Bernardo died around 1992. Some drug dealers he brought into his home tied him up and robbed him; he wriggled loose and tried to escape through his apartment building's second-floor window, but he plummeted and fell on top of a gas meter, which, like a spike, impaled him, slicing right through one of his vital organs. I was heartbroken, of course, but I knew by then that he was HIV positive—and that AIDS, just like with Jobriath, would kill him sooner or later. Back then, HIV was a death sentence. So I took some solace in the belief that by going out this way, quickly, Bernardo had been spared some suffering.

But by 1992, I was too busy being a full-blown crack addict and running around with the infamous Arthur Lee, anyway.

There was no band in Los Angeles, or anywhere, like Arthur Lee's Love in the 1960s. They ruled the Sunset Strip; they were integrated; and Arthur's lyrics were pure poetry to me. Love was the first LA band I adored when I touched down in Hollywood. Every jukebox that got my spare change played Love, Love, Love: "A Message to Pretty," "My Little Red Book," "You Set the Scene." Love's *Forever Changes* is still one of my top ten albums.

The first time I actually met Arthur was around 1970. I was at the Hollywood apartment that I shared with Marlowe B. West and Marquise, and Devon Wilson, a.k.a. Dolly Dagger, Jimi Hendrix's girlfriend, had come over. She and her friends knocked on my door and said, "We're looking for Mercy. We were sent here by Keith Richards so you can take us to Gram Parsons's place so we can get high." Jimi was dead by this point, and for some reason Devon brought in a bunch of Jimi's clothes and hung them in my closet. We went off hitchhiking in the direction of the Chateau Marmont, and along the way John Astin, a.k.a. Gomez Addams himself, picked us up and we smoked a joint with him. He was a cool dude. But I digress. My point is, Arthur was part of Devon's entourage that afternoon.

Arthur was a wild-eyed guy, so tall and so handsome, but so totally fucked up. He was so loaded that he hid in my bathroom and claimed the boogeyman was after him. At that point in my life, I thought to myself, "Damn, this guy's a little *too* freaky, even for me." I had immense respect for Arthur as a musician, but I didn't feel the need to hang with him right then. It takes a lot to scare me, but he scared the crap out of me.

When Arthur and I finally hooked up a couple decades later, that boogeyman had followed him all the way into the nineties. That damn monster was still chasing him. I believe it chased him till the day he died.

It was around 1990 that our paths crossed again. I was still scared of Arthur, but not enough to stay away this time—even though he was truly the last person I needed in my life, with my raging crack habit that I was half-heartedly trying to kick. I was working as a housekeeper for a woman named Jonna—who'd been an original, short-lived GTO back in the day and had given birth to Lowell George's son, Forrest—and one night Arthur came sauntering into Jonna's condo with Miss Lucy. It was Arthur's birthday and he'd recently gotten out of jail, and he'd almost gotten arrested again while he was driving Lucy, who had AIDS by this point and would die a year later, to the free clinic.

I got one eyeful of Arthur and gasped: "*Oh. My. God.*"

Despite the hard life he had led, with drugs and prison and all that, Arthur looked like aging should. He was still so gorgeous. And he seemed less insane this time. He was polite, very different from our previous encounter twenty years earlier. Arthur stared real hard at me, because I was looking a whole lot better than I did back in my chubby GTOs days, and he flipped out, raving, "Wow, you're *incredible!*" I knew then and there that I wanted a relationship with him...even when he started smoking crack right in front of me.

However, Arthur ended up going off with Jonna. She was really attracted to him and she went straight for him, so I sat back, since it wasn't my style to try to poach a girlfriend's boyfriend. We all began hanging out together, but I was keeping my feelings away, and Arthur was keeping *his* feelings away. Jonna was giving him a lot of sex, and it was obvious she was in love with him, really gaga over him—but whenever we'd go to Arthur's recording sessions, he was always flirting with me.

One night when I sleeping over at Jonna's house, Arthur decided to climb into bed with me. He tried to pretend he was high and it was an accident, but trust me, it was no accident. Jonna caught him and flew into a jealous rage, so he confessed to her, "I want to sleep with Mercy." She wigged out some more, and then she tossed us out.

I protested: "Hey! I didn't invite him to get in bed with me. I didn't ask him to. That's just what he did. Why are you throwing both of us out? This isn't my fault!" But she would not listen to reason, so that is when I decided to just go for it with Arthur. I felt no more loyalty to Jonna. Arthur and I took off and checked into a motel for days and days.

The relationship wasn't especially sexual for me. Arthur thought our motel sex was great; I didn't think it was so great. When he would take me to his sessions, oh, my God—*that* was great. The romance for me was more in that I adored him as person, and as a musician. But Arthur just liked sex and crack; he was a man of simple needs. He would even try to make me watch hardcore pornography while I cooked up our crack. That was our domestic scene. It was pure madness.

One night in the studio, Arthur and I had rabbit-like jackhammer sex for hours and hours, and I was so sore the next day that I couldn't even walk. And he was raving, "Wow, wasn't it amazing?"

And I grumbled, "No, not really." I never had a big sexual thing for Arthur. Doing crack actually makes a woman fairly asexual. It makes a man extremely oversexed, to the point that he can never get enough, but it had the opposite effect on me.

One time when Arthur and I were over at Gary Leonard's place, Jonna called up Gary and screamed, "Where's my boyfriend? Why does Mercy have him?" And she drove over to try to drag Arthur out of Gary's house. She wanted him back so badly. I do think Arthur was having sex with her on the side.

Another time we were visiting her and she started giving him head, and Arthur said, "See, Mercy, *this* is the way you're supposed to do it," because doing that was never my big thing. He ordered me, "Just cook the rocks and be quiet," so there I was in the kitchen at the stove, putting in baking soda and cocaine together and serving them rocks, and he was sitting on the sofa, oohing and aahing with Jonna kneeling between his legs: "Yeah, yeah, *this* is the way you're supposed to do it." It made me sick. It was always a bizarre scene with Arthur, it really was.

Jonna eventually went certifiably nuts. Years later I ran into her and she was holding a photograph of Jimi Hendrix in her hand, stating real calmly and factually, "This is my husband." She was babbling about how she was married to Jimi, who was of course long dead. I went back with her to her condo, and it was a total wreck. She explained that the police had just been there to investigate a domestic disturbance because she'd had a bad fight with Jimi. This is how crazy she got. Later she moved to Seattle to be closer to her "in-laws." She used to have arguments with her hand.

Arthur and I would go on crack binges, living in and out of motels, usually with our best buddy, the great psychedelic garage rock wizard Sky Saxon, along for the ride. Sky, Arthur, and I were a threesome—we never had sex together, it was never like *that*, but Sky was always with us. Sky was as cracked up as Arthur was, and he dabbled in plenty of other substances, too. Once Sky and I went dancing and he gave me this pill; I took it and it was real acid, which I had not realized. A couple days later, I found out from a *High Times* cover story that Sky was a member of this LSD cult in Hawaii. But most of the time, the three of us just smoked crack together; that was our main scene. We'd smoke, go to one of Arthur's sessions, and then Sky would have a session—and that's where I'd first heard Arthur on the keyboards. I had no idea that Arthur was this incredible soul brother dude who could play all this Chitlin' Circuit music.

One time I was staying over at Sky's, and Arthur decided out of the blue that I had to leave, that I couldn't be over there. He burst in and chucked all my clothes out into the street. I have no idea why he did that. Maybe he was jealous, but nothing was going on between me and Sky. Arthur kind of owned me, or at least acted like he owned me. He wasn't violent most of the time—though I did slap him once. I can't recall why; I just got stupid and slapped him in the supermarket. I didn't blacken his eye or anything. Slapping somebody is a little different than punching them. Slapping has just always been my thing. I slap people, that's what I do.

The only time I was ever scared of Arthur was when he was fucked up and would fall asleep while driving. He was always on some medication on top of the crack and whatever else he was doing. That would kick my autophobia right back into high gear, no pun intended. Arthur was another guy that had me jumping out of cars all the time—he'd nod out behind the wheel, and I'd plot my escape. That's why we rarely were seen out in public as a couple. We almost went to a club together once, but he fell asleep at the wheel at Fairfax and Sunset.

One time we were cruising around and passed by the Rhino Records building. Arthur screeched the car to a halt and said, "I'm going to talk to them. I'm going to get that damn man!"—the man that ran the Rhino record label, I assumed, though I'm not sure exactly who. Arthur left me in the car. He was going to go in there and just go cause a huge scene—something to do with a reissue or whatever. But he came back after being informed that the label president wasn't there. He was hysterical over this. He probably would've beat the fuck out of that guy.

Such behavior was typical of Arthur. He tried to cause a similar scene at B.B. King's Blues Club on Universal CityWalk many years later. Pamela and I went to B.B. King's joint shortly after Arthur got out of jail again, for Jimi Hendrix's sixtieth birthday bash concert. Jimi's brother Leon and surprise guest Buddy Miles were also playing, and Buddy and Arthur were fighting over who was officially headlining. Arthur thought he should get top billing; Buddy thought he should. They had been dear friends, but they'd been involved in some dope deal years before and Arthur felt like he'd gotten burned. He was all ready to go downstairs and beat the fuck out of Buddy, but then he saw Buddy was in a wheelchair. So he went, "Fuck, I can't beat him up."

Arthur wasn't talking to me, and he threw Pamela out of his dressing room. (Arthur hated Pamela because he quite wrongly believed that she was prejudiced—he thought she didn't date Black guys, which was 100 percent untrue. Pamela actually liked Arthur quite a bit. Before he died, Arthur called up Pamela and said, "I hope you forgive me. But if you don't, fuck you." That's exactly what he said. That was his goodbye.) So Arthur didn't beat up Buddy that night, thankfully. But when Arthur was onstage, everybody started screaming for Buddy, which clearly irritated Arthur. And by the way, Arthur talked shit about Jimi while he was onstage, to boot.

Arthur really was too much. He was bad news. Even Robert Plant was scared of him. I remember I was with Robert Plant at one of his gigs, and Robert was doing Love songs. I offered to introduce him to Arthur, but Robert said, "No, I really don't want to meet him. I don't want to know him. I just want to do his songs." Robert didn't want that illusion shattered. Arthur's reputation was *so* bad at this point. Arthur Lee genuinely *scared* people. However, everyone respected his talent. When Robert later found out that Arthur had leukemia and there was a fundraiser in New York, Robert actually flew in from London to do it.

Arthur and I dated on and off for about a year, until the day we got stopped by the cops. And then we were *off*, at least for a little while.

That day, Arthur picked me up and informed me that we were going to the "ghetto side" of town to score crack. His cousin, who was in the backseat, looked me over with trepidation and said to me, "Oh, *you're* the girl Arthur's always talking about. You're the one that's messing his head up."

I just shrugged and said, "Okay, whatever."

As we were driving, Arthur already seemed super paranoid and told me, "If they pull us over, I'm walking."

Well, we got pulled over, naturally. Seriously, Arthur's entire life seemed to be a series of police traffic stops.

True to his word, Arthur began walking away from the car. He just got out of the driver's seat and started walking. And you don't really do that with cops, especially if you're a Black man—you could get killed. As he was walking away, the cops yanked my rollers out of my hair to see if I had any drugs hidden in them. Luckily my hairdo was crack-free that day since we had been on our way to *get* drugs. I was trying to do something to stop what was happening, so I said to the officers, "Do you *know* who this is? This is Arthur Lee!" And I sang "My Little Red Book," or *tried* to sing it.

The cop gasped, "Wow, you're kidding me!"

The policeman then looked up Arthur's rap sheet, which of course was horrible and about ten miles long. But the cop must have been a secret Love fan, because he called out to Arthur, "Come back here. You'll be okay. Don't worry." And he told Arthur, "I'm going to let you go, but I'm taking your cousin in because he's got a warrant out, and we're seizing your car." It was actually Arthur's other girlfriend Diane's car. Diane was the one Arthur ended up marrying in 2006, the year he died, because she was a nurse. She was always there for him.

And finally, before the cop let us go, he scolded me: "You shouldn't go out with guys that have this kind of rap sheet."

After this was all over, Arthur and I walked in stony silence to a nearby McDonald's. As we sat there with our not-so-happy meals, Arthur blurted out, "This is the end of us. We're done now. We've got to end this relationship. It brings nothing but trouble." He said we were a bad combination, and I couldn't really argue with him. "Yeah, maybe you're right," I said.

But soon after that, Arthur was calling me again, and he came over in this really fancy car. I was now roommates with Don Johnson—not the famous *Miami Vice* actor that Pamela used to date, but a gay guy named Don Johnson. I pretended to be with Don (I kind of *did* want to be with Don, to be honest) because I didn't want to get back into it with Arthur. But Arthur dispatched me to MacArthur Park to buy some crack, and I couldn't say no to him. He handed me $100 and dropped me off on my errand. Afterward, I refused to get back in his car, in broad daylight, right in front of this drug-infested park. I told him, "If you think I'm going to score drugs and step into this Lexus, you are insane. Are you just screaming for me to go to jail or what?" So I took the money, copped the crack, hopped on a bus, and then I called Arthur later that evening and interrupted his dinner with Diane. I said, "I have your drugs, okay? I didn't try to rip you off. I'm a woman of my word." Arthur came over after dinner to smoke crack with me, and that's how we started up again. But we both knew it couldn't last.

While I was dating Arthur, I rang up Shuggie, whom I was on good terms with at the time, and insisted to him, "You've *got* to come meet Arthur!" They'd met years earlier, when Shuggie was a teenager, and Shuggie idolized Arthur, really respected him. There were very few people that Shuggie felt that way about. I'd always felt like Shuggie's "Strawberry Letter 23" and Arthur's "Orange Skies" were kindred-spirit songs. So I reunited them in the nineties, and they actually ended up playing together for a bit. That was my networking skills at work, and I was proud of that.

Arthur didn't last long out of jail before he went back for shooting off a gun in his apartment. I think he was still always looking for the boogeyman. This time he was imprisoned for about six years, under the "three strikes" law. But I saw him from time to time after he was released in 2001.

The last time I saw Arthur was not long before he died. My girlfriend Jill and I went over to his house in the San Fernando Valley, and he was not feeling well. Love's already-booked UK tour had gone on without him, and he was angry that his relatively new backing band, the guys from the LA power-pop combo Baby Lemonade, had done that—even though they had no choice because there was a contract to fulfill. Arthur was watching OutKast's "Hey Ya!" music video over and again, asking us, "Do you like this guy?" And I said,

"Yeah, that cat is pretty darn cool." Arthur nodded. Evidently, he also thought Andre 3000 was cool.

Arthur told us that day, "I wrote a book, but I don't know who I gave it to. I had my story all written in jail." So somewhere, there is an unpublished Arthur Lee memoir that exists. Then he asked me, "I want to sell some of my stuff. Can I give it to you to sell? I don't feel very well, and I want to sell this, I'll sell that, that, that"—babbling and pointing to random objects in his home. And then he hit on Jill, right in front of me. He said to her, "Can you spend the night? Don't worry. I can't do anything." She declined, of course.

Weirdly, I asked Arthur to sign two autographs for me before Jill and I said goodbye. I had a premonition. After we left, I said to Jill, "This is the last time I'm ever going to see him alive. I know this. I'm never going to see Arthur again. I'm not going to see that man on this planet anymore." I sold the autographs later. I had no use for them anymore. By that time, Arthur and I had been through so much that I didn't need anything to remember him by. But I did really love him.

I went by Arthur's house sometime later to check up on him, but he had moved out. I called him and it was forwarded to a number in Memphis. He picked up and said, "Mercy, I'm in the doctor's waiting room right now. I have leukemia. And by the way, I married Diane. She's a nurse. I'm going to beat this." He was doing stem cell therapy, which I found out about later. But he didn't beat it.

Diane had Arthur's body transported back to Forest Lawn Memorial Park in Los Angeles. She denied that I'd had any connection with Arthur and was furious when I gave a speech at his service ("You spoke at the funeral because *anybody* could speak at the funeral," she later told me, coldly), but she was just grieving, and I understood. At the funeral I merely gushed about what a musical genius Arthur was and didn't get into anything salacious or personal. It was a terrible experience for me, to be honest, because they brought a damn bulldozer in and unceremoniously dropped Arthur's coffin into a hole in the ground. Then they released some doves, which was lovely, but to see the open grave of my friend, like it was some sort of construction site, was *not* fun. I wish I had not seen that. I thought I had gotten over Arthur long ago, but in that moment, I realized I would never get over him.

14

The Eureka Springs Garbage Lady

I MET MY SECOND husband, in the early nineties, over a rock. It wasn't a diamond. This was a different kind of engagement rock.

I first saw Leonard standing between two Hollywood apartment houses. He was just my type: Black, fit, good-looking. I asked if he had any crack for sale, and he gave me a very good deal—a twenty-dollar rock for just five bucks. I thought, "Wow, that's pretty cool." I would pay the real price later.

Leonard and I became an item soon after that. He was hip and really quite bright, and he'd had a good upbringing. He had fallen—or maybe been pushed—out of a six-story window and had been in a wheelchair for three months, and he'd just gotten out of a rehabilitation center before I met him. Apparently doing crack helped him walk, or so he claimed. I had no idea about any of this until I saw him one time crawling on the floor and realized he was pretty screwed up. I think the reason he smoked crack had a lot to do with pain. When he was high, his pain didn't exist. Isn't that why anyone does any drug, really? It's all about some sort of pain management.

I kind of loved Leonard, I suppose. I loved him for what the situation was. It wasn't a big fantasy show. There was no white wedding; we just went down to City Hall. We became financially stuck together, and at some point in the marriage, that became Leonard's only appeal for me. That was part of the attraction in the beginning, too, but I *was* attracted to him; we shared an undeniable chemistry. I was so addicted to crack—and, by association, to Leonard—that I put up with all his crap.

Leonard was charming at first, but it didn't take long before all that changed. I can't remember when he first hit me—if it was before we got married, that would be pretty stupid of me, but I honestly don't know. All I know is one time he just hauled up and bashed the fuck out of me. We weren't having a fight, nothing like that; we were just sitting in our house with some friends and out of nowhere, he slugged me. I looked at him like a confused puppy, my throbbing head tilted to one side, as if to say, "Huh? What the hell? Why did you just do that?" I was shocked more than anything else.

I ran outside and sat on the stoop, trying to calm down and process what had just happened. Leonard followed me and I thought, "Oh, cool, here he comes to apologize." But then he punched me again. I didn't know him that well, but I thought, "Well, I guess I'll forgive him after this." You might have assumed that I would've walked out on him, but I honestly had nowhere else to go, and I didn't know another life at that point.

I would never know when Leonard was going to hit me. He was like a damn boxer. Once we were smoking crack for hours, and he hit me so hard that he bashed in the entire side of my face. I was so high that I didn't realize how badly I'd been injured; I didn't feel the pain. Then I went to survey the damage in the mirror, and half my face was gone, completely sunken in. Leonard had broken all the bones in the side of my face. Somehow I made it to the hospital and got it fixed. I had no money for it; the government footed the bill. The surgeon had to pull out all the shattered shards of my face and put me back together again like Humpty Dumpty, and he said he'd never seen anything like it, had never seen anything so broken. Supposedly they put my eyeball on the table for a while and then popped it back in, or so I was told. The damage Leonard did to me was crazy. I'm still scarred like a football player, and part of my face is all metal now and totally asymmetrical. But the doctor did a pretty good job, considering what he had left to work with.

I went over to Pamela's house to recover, and I stayed away from Leonard for a bit after that, but eventually I went back to him. I honestly don't know why. He would always point to the busted side of my face, to my misshapen eye socket, and make fun of me. Maybe I believed no one would ever find me attractive again, so I might as well stick with the one man who'd have me.

I was still connected to Pamela through all this. She accepted my lifestyle, but she worried a lot, and she'd dispatch her artist friend Victor Hayden—a.k.a. the Mascara Snake, who was Captain Beefheart's cousin—to find me on the streets and make sure I wasn't dead. Along with Pamela and Victor, I had a few other dear allies looking out for me. One time when Leonard was beating me outside, splaying me across a car in the middle of Argyle Avenue as he pummeled me, the soul singer Spyder Turner, who lived across the street, came running out with a baseball bat, shouting, "Don't you ever hit her again!"

When Shuggie heard about what was going on with Leonard, he and Teri even called me and said, "Leave the dude. We'll deal with him. We'll do something." They sounded so frantic and concerned, and it was nice to realize Shuggie still cared. He and Lucky once showed up to one of my temporary apartments because I would never answer the phone, but then Shuggie walked in and said with relief, "Oh, you look great." I wasn't actually doing great.

　　　　　　　Mercy Fontenot *and* Lyndsey Parker

Arthur Lee once came to visit me too. He gave Leonard a pistol, just for fun. Yep, that's what the crack days were like! Arthur was watching himself on a VHS tape, over and over. He'd just come back from Liverpool, from a show that had been a smashing success, and he was very high on that. "Everybody knows my songs! Everybody knows me!" he kept raving. Arthur seemed less concerned about my well-being than my other ex, Shuggie, had.

Sometimes I would go stay by myself at the local Catholic church when things got real bad with Leonard, because I knew he couldn't come there. But I was still getting high. No, the nuns wouldn't get high with me—I had a little dorm room, and I would smoke some crack and then go downstairs and face the sisters, acting all innocent. It was crazy.

Leonard and I were homeless off and on a lot during our marriage. We had no home. We smoked ourselves out of our homes, in and out of apartments. We'd get an apartment and then end up using all the rent money for dope. But honestly, it wasn't that bad. I felt like a Gypsy much of the time.

I had this joke: "When I got married, I thought I'd be pushing a baby carriage, not a shopping cart!" But the homeless crackhead lifestyle could actually be a ton of fun. In a weird way, I idolized the idea of Skid Row because of that Bob Dylan song, "Desolation Row." So I chose being homeless. I *chose* that life. I thought it'd be an interesting experience—and it was, for a while.

Our little crackhead community was united. Nobody shared their rocks, of course; crack is a very selfish drug. It's not a "hey, you want to come to a rock party?" or pass-the-pipe-around sort of drug. Everyone was like a little squirrel with its own little nut. But we all got along well and watched each other's backs. I never felt unsafe— except with my husband. Leonard was the only thing that scared me.

At that time, I had a general relief check and Leonard had his disability check, and that was our base, but we had to get creative when it came to other ways of earning money. I never considered prostitution, even though that would have been the obvious solution. It just wasn't in my realm—I mean, if I didn't enjoy sex with rock 'n' roll stars, why would I try to do it with regular johns? So Leonard and I earned a bit on the side by getting in business with this shifty dude that sold bootleg concert T-shirts in front of the Hollywood Palladium. But really how we made our honest living was from recycling—we were helping the environment while helping ourselves to as much crack as we could get.

We had no rules, no ties, no schedule. We were totally off the grid. I absolutely loved it. Every morning I'd get up, push my cart up and down the Hollywood streets, get a bunch of exercise, and nobody bothered me. I rarely got in trouble, and found all sorts of treasures digging around in the trash. I even ate out of garbage cans; I used to go down to the Jack in the Box and dig in the dumpsters, and that would be my dinner. Of course, if I wanted quick drug money for a fix, I'd grab bottles and cans, but along with that, I'd find that people threw away all sorts of collectibles: amazing albums, costume jewelry, vintage clothes that I could resell on Melrose Avenue. Books were a big racket for me. I dug up an original Iceberg Slim autographed novel and got about $100 for that, and another time I found a whole bin full of rare books and got a couple hundred dollars for that from an antique bookstore. I picked up many street skills that helped me later on, once I went straight and got a legitimate job as an auction curator for Goodwill's Hollywood flagship store. I learned how to make money from trash.

One day during my street adventures I was pushing my cart past the Pantages Theater on Hollywood Boulevard, and I spotted my old pal Rodney the Rooster strutting in. I rolled right up to Rod Stewart and called out, "Hey, it's Mercy!" I was much thinner, and much older, but I'm pretty sure he recognized me. Obviously Rod was still full of himself because he hurried into the theater, giving me a quick wave and a nod and moving right along. I am sure I was *supposed* to be embarrassed, like I was *supposed* to think, "Oh, no, Rod is this millionaire rock star now and I'm this pathetic, homeless drug addict!" But why should I be ashamed? I wasn't. Shame isn't really something I do. Plus, I always looked cute when I was pushing a shopping cart. I wasn't some rag-hag. I still had some style. I was still *me*.

I don't think I ever hit my rock bottom. Maybe I'm still waiting for it! But to me, "rock bottom" is when you lose everything, and I didn't feel I had. I was having fun, enjoying my free-ranging Gypsy existence. Plus, I was still living this double celebrity life with Pamela and her fancy friends. One day I'd be homeless, smoking crack on the streets and eating my dumpster dinner, and then the next day I'd walk into some glamorous soiree at Pamela's house filled with celebrities like Michael Hutchence and Christina Applegate.

One night during this time, Pamela, Christina, Michael, and Michael's stylist, Lynn Bugatti, and I all went to Ice-T's club in Hollywood. When nobody was looking, a bodyguard kept dragging me over to Ice's velvet-roped VIP table, saying stuff to him like, "Here is your present!"

I kept tearing away; I was not at all interested in Ice-T. I was trying to tell Pamela, but she wouldn't listen and said to me, exasperated, "Why are you acting like an idiot?"

Michael noticed what was going on and intervened, saying, "Mercy, come with me." And he put me in a car and rescued me. We spent the whole night talking until five in the morning, and I was so grateful for his help.

Michael Hutchence was a sweetheart and a truly special person. He had a bit of Jim Morrison, a bit of Mick Jagger, in him. He was an old soul, and there was definitely some of that old-school magic about him. But he had a bad drug habit, especially with cocaine, and he died under mysterious circumstances only a few years after we met. Michael was always incredibly kind to me. When I was in trouble and once again didn't have a place to live, he sent me some rent money so I could go get a place. I ended up crashing temporarily with a local punk-funk band called Liquid Jesus, and after a night of hanging with Michael, he drove me back to their apartment. I walked in and announced, "I was just with Michael Hutchence from INXS! He just dropped me off!" They did not believe me, of course. I was leading such a dual life—a homeless crack addict by day who partied with celebrities at Ice-T's joint by night.

This became eight years of my life. I would go to Pamela's on and off, and she always accepted me. But I did take a ring from her once, as well as some CDs. That is one of the few things I've done in my life that I am genuinely ashamed of. I didn't usually steal from my friends, but I was at the height of my crack addiction, and she was leaving me alone in her house, so something like that was bound to happen. However, there is no excuse. When I confessed to this crime years later, it only made things worse. Pamela had always had this faith in me, and her girlfriend Catherine James, another famous rock muse, had warned her: "You know, you can't trust Mercy." And then I went and proved Catherine right. It deeply hurt Pamela's feelings. Maybe there are some things I should just stay quiet about.

I did all the dumb shit that crack addicts do. Once I sold Lucky's CDs, though of course I hated those CDs because they were heavy metal and I didn't want my son listening to them anyway. The other time I thieved from a friend was when I was living with the gay Don Johnson. He became furious with me for selling his radio, and in his rage he pushed me and I fell and tore a ligament in my leg. I ended up on crutches for a month and a half. This was right around the time that Lucky had somehow made it through high school, so I had to attend his graduation ceremony at Belmont High with a cast on my leg. Shuggie, Johnny, and Phyllis were not impressed. Lucky, of course, knew what was up. I may not have realized that he had been smoking pot since he was fifteen, but he was well aware of my addiction. When you're doing crack, people *know* you're doing crack.

I wound up in jail a few times. I got arrested for being under the influence when I wasn't even under the influence—I guess I just looked the part. I was a "threat to normalcy," as Pamela would put it. Once I was walking to get a cup of coffee, and the cops drove up on me and said, "You're under arrest!" The transient motel Leonard and I were staying at then was notorious for that. Another time I got arrested when I bought crack from an undercover cop in MacArthur Park. It was total entrapment, but I spent a couple of days in the clink.

People have asked me why I stayed with Leonard for so long. Yes, a lot of it was financial, but also I got used to having somebody around. I kept thinking he was going to get better, that the situation might get better. But when I found out I could be something on my own, with my own job and my sobriety, that ended that. I never wanted to see that environment around me again, never wanted to be there again, never wanted to go to jail again. I got tired of living this life, just like I'd gotten tired of being Shuggie's housewife.

People have also asked me which substance—crack, speed, heroin, cigarettes—was the hardest for me to quit. But really, none of it was hard. It was harder to *stay* on it. Crack was especially easy to quit since it wasn't physically addicting for me. It was emotionally addicting; the fun was in the chase of getting the crack. The high was all in my head. But at some point I could see the future and what my life was going to be, and it was fairly easy for me to say no to that. I was sober by the age of fifty.

I got sober on Thanksgiving Day 1998. I was living with my German landlady during yet another rift with Leonard, and she kept scolding me for getting high. She had once been married to a member of the 18th Street gang and wouldn't let me do crack in her apartment, so I had hidden my pipe outside by the garbage can in my usual smoking spot. That day I couldn't find my pipe, and as I was frantically rummaging through the alley trash in search of it, I suddenly said to myself, "That's it. That's fucking *it*. I'm going to AA." And I stomped over to an AA meeting, literally across the street, and never picked up the pipe again.

Those meetings were filled with celebrities. Seriously, if you're a groupie, go to Alcoholics Anonymous or Narcotics Anonymous. But NA wasn't a working program for me. It felt like too dark a place. It was better for me to be away from those meetings and not think about it rather than be surrounded by people who were deep in their own addictions, listen to their crazy, rock-bottom stories, and then find out that they'd fatally overdosed the very next day. So ultimately, I quit all by myself. I just knew I needed to do it.

The only good thing that came out of my marriage to Leonard is we eventually got sober together. He started working at Goodwill, and I followed him over there and I got the job that I still have to this day, more than twenty years later, so I have to thank Leonard for that. Things were good for a while. We even had our own cute apartment. But then we went to Las Vegas on some sort of morale-boosting, team-building Goodwill staff trip, and he disappeared. He never got on the bus to go home, and I was freaking out, thinking somebody had kidnapped or even killed him. Then I got a call from the credit card bureau saying his card was being flagged for suspicious charges, and that made me even more paranoid.

Leonard turned up at our place a few days later with some prostitute that he knew from our crack days, and it was obvious that he'd gone back to his old demonic ways. I had started noticing the warning signs a bit before that—not that he hit me again, thank God, but he started disappearing a lot. I figured out that he was using, so I got the hell away from him and moved into Pamela's house, where I stayed for the next four years. This time, Leonard and I were over for good; if you're not a user, you simply cannot be with a user. So I kept working at Goodwill, Leonard got fired, and we just parted. And that's how that ended. Leonard was never able to kick drugs, and he died five years later, in October 2003.

I wanted so badly to make it up to Pamela for all the heartache I had caused her. Pamela's mother, Margaret, became ill, and Pamela would have to go away on business trips, so I became Margaret's caretaker, dedicating two and a half years of my life to that sweet woman. In some ways, as odd as it may sound, this was a wonderful time in my life. It felt good to be there for Pamela and her mother, and I had so much fun when I was trundling her around in her wheelchair.

Unfortunately, Pamela's mom grew sicker. I was the one to unofficially diagnose Margaret. I could hear a rattle, something really deep within her frail body, eerily emanating from her chest, and I said, "Listen, we need to take her somewhere. I hear something." It turned out she had a tumor in her lung. It was lung cancer.

Margaret had smoked like a fiend for decades, and at the end of her life she was phantom-smoking—in other words, she was smoking, but there was no cigarette in her hand. She was going through the motions, like some sort of chain-smoking mime, even when she was asleep. To see that spooked me, and that got me off of cigarettes, which was one of my last lingering addictions. I took one last puff, and that was it. I didn't use a patch or gum or anything like that.

And at the very end, when Margaret was under hospice care, there was morphine all around. And I didn't touch any of it. There was a time in my past when I totally would have. But I stayed sober because I had a *reason* to stay sober, which was to help this dear lady and help my friend. Pamela would have *never* let me take care of her mother while I was stoned, believe me, and I'd only been clean for about a month and a half when I took on these important nursemaid duties—so to be given that sort of responsibility and that trust was so very special to me.

It made me want to be different. It made me want to be better. Everything in my life became new.

15

Knockin' on Heaven's Door

RIGHT AFTER DARBY CRASH of the Germs died, I was walking down Cahuenga and ran into Rodney Bingenheimer. He said to me, "You know, we're the only ones left." That was 1980, and we're both still here. We'll see how much longer I get.

I was living with Pamela and working at Goodwill when I found out from the free clinic that I had hepatitis C, which I probably contracted from shooting drugs; everyone shared needles back in the day like it was nothing, which was really stupid. The doctors were all very matter-of-fact when giving me my damning diagnosis. They told me there was no cure—that it would eventually progress and turn into cirrhosis and then liver cancer, and that slowly but surely this would kill me. "Your liver is just going to shut down," they warned.

So I figured, "Well, if I've I only got few years left, let me have some fun."

And that's where the gambling came in. Gambling was my final vice. I had given up drugs and smoking and everything else, so of course I needed a new hobby. I am sure this was yet another compulsion I inherited from my parents. In fact, if my mom and dad had been alive at this time, they probably would've been right there next to me in the casinos.

My gambling addiction started with one of my Vegas trips with the Goodwill team when on a whim I slipped seventy-five cents into a slot machine and pushed a couple buttons, and it started chirping, "You're in the money!" And $3,000 came spewing out.

I thought, "Gee, this is fun." And it was fun, at first. Back in LA, I was soon hitting up every local casino whenever I could. It was just some place to go; there was no club scene really or anything for me at that time. I could spend $300 in a couple hours just on the penny slots. My thinking was, "I'm going to be dead soon, so what's the difference? I don't have to pay this money back." Just like my dad in his final days, I didn't give a fuck anymore. I figured I'd been handed a death sentence, so I wanted to do anything to have a good time and get my mind off things.

The bad news is, I lost enough money that I'm still actually paying off the debt. But the good news is, obviously I am still alive.

Around 2013, my liver doctor told me, "There's a new miracle cure on the horizon. And when we get it, we're going to cure you." I got excited...until I found out that it was $1,000 a pill, called Harvoni. It was a $90,000 treatment. When I found out about the cost, I started sobbing. "That's ridiculous," I cried. "I can't afford that!" But then this doctor, yet another one of my guardian angels, told me, "Don't worry, you don't have to pay anything. We'll get you Medical Financial Assistance." And in about five weeks, I was cured of my hep C.

Later I was, in fact, diagnosed with liver cancer, and it has come back a few times. It's always a teeny tiny little speck, and the surgeons slice it out and I'm okay for a while, but it eventually returns. The strange, funny thing about what I'm going through now is how so many medical procedures remind me of when I was doing drugs. Like when I get a CAT scan, I get the same damn rush that oozes from my head through my sex organs because of the iodine injections. It takes me right back to the first time I ever shot up meth in Laguna Beach. Or sometimes I recall how fun I used to think it was to shoot up, but then I started having to inject myself with interferon, bringing syringes home and shooting myself in the leg four times a week for a year, and now I don't enjoy the needle at all anymore. I also think about how when people would visit me in the hospital, I wanted to keep doing morphine so I'd look good. I felt just like Sister Morphine. Luckily I felt no addiction to it once the pain had passed. Some people might find it odd that this didn't trigger any relapse. But all my addictions are long gone. I don't take handfuls of anything anymore. Drugs are a different thing for me now. But I do think it's ironic that I ended up this way.

Lucky hasn't been around during any of my recent health scares, but he knows everything. Whenever I'm recuperating from an operation, I'll get a phone call from one of his girlfriends asking how I'm doing, and I'll know Lucky put her up to that. Lucky never talks for himself. But something truly wonderful has come out of all this. Another angel was sent my way. In 2018, I found some new family—a niece, Kniqui, that I'd never known about before. I received a private Facebook message that said, "Do you know this woman Sandra? Is she your sister? Because that's my mother." I couldn't believe what I was reading. So I called my other niece, whom I'm very close with, and I said, "Um, do you have a sister?" And she said, "Yes, I do, but my mother gave her up years ago, and we never found her." And I said, "Well, she just found me!"

Kniqui, my long-lost niece, and I got on the phone and we had an instant bond, as if we'd known each other all our lives. We were immediately best friends. She even came to LA to take care of me after one of my cancer procedures, and even put us up in the swanky W

Hotel in Hollywood, this rock 'n' roll hotel that costs $300 a day, and she stayed by my side for a week. I think that helped me immensely. If I would've been in any kind of stressful situation, things could have taken a darker turn. Maybe the surgery wouldn't have worked. But I was feeling fantastic within two days, thanks to Kniqui. She is pretty damn fabulous. And we are truly family now.

Recently I got another spot in a different place that was too close to the heart for the docs to do anything except chemo. Location, location, location, right? They shrunk it down to hardly anything, but they couldn't do the radiation to make it go away entirely because it was too close to the vein. Now, it's getting bigger; it has grown to the size of a dime. So I guess I really am permanently damaged now. I'm just trying to keep myself alive. For some reason, I have faith that it's going to work. Maybe I will get a good five years. I figure that's all I need.

I actually really enjoy the life that I'm living today. Working full-time at my age, with my many health issues, is tough and can be exhausting, but I love my life. I love going to see my son perform, I love Pamela's parties, I love meeting new people and getting back in touch with old friends and family on Facebook. I like *now*. I think my life is God-sent. And most of all, I am so grateful that I can still get excited about new musical discoveries; I'm far from jaded when it comes to that.

My latest, and possibly final, passion is Yoshiki, from the phenomenally successful glam-metal band X Japan. When I saw him speak at a Grammy Museum event, I had no idea who he was or what I was walking into. But when he glided onto the stage, a little slip of a man-child in sleek black leather and wraparound shades, I sensed an aura around him that was different from that of any rock musician I'd ever encountered before. It was a step beyond. I could not believe I had not known about this ethereal creature before. He was such a crossover. It was like looking at a woman. I found out he'd been on the cover of *Vogue Japan*, the first man to have that honor. He was this stunning, high-cheekboned diva boy, much like the ones I used to love and follow around in the sixties and seventies. He definitely had that unisex thing going on.

And then, to find out that Yoshiki is also an accomplished, genius classical musician and composer—well, after that, I spent all my time obsessing, intensely wishing and praying that I could meet him. I knew I needed to meet this person before I died. And so, I meditated on it, just like I used to. It was not a sexual thing—Yoshiki is fine as hell, but I'm over seventy years old, so let's be realistic here. I merely wanted to bask in his aura. And then I scored an invitation to his classical performance at the opening of the Japan House in Hollywood. I was sitting at my VIP table, yelling his name, and I am sure his publicist was weirded out, but I could not contain myself. I felt seventeen again. I was bursting with joy.

And then, suddenly, Yoshiki floated over to our table. I actually knew he would. It felt like he was another vision I had seen in a dream and this was supposed to happen, or I had willed it to happen. I said, "Hello, I'm Miss Mercy. I used to be in the GTOs with Frank Zappa. I've met a lot of famous rock stars, but I have never, ever in my lifetime been so amazed by somebody that I think is so above it all." I'm not sure if he understood what I was saying, but he said with a little formal bow, "Oh, that's really nice," very cordial and very sweet. And very fabulous. I was just happy that at my age, I could still be so over the moon for someone.

Whatever happens next, I know I've made my mark. For instance, I know Courtney Love adored me and the GTOs. Don Bolles told me that Courtney used to follow me everywhere, that she was obsessed with me. Courtney said she wanted to portray me if there was ever a movie made about the GTOs. Once when I was staying with Pamela,

I answered the phone and this girl said, "Hi, my name is Courtney Love, and I want to play Miss Mercy in *I'm with the Band*"—which was supposed to be a movie starring Ally Sheedy, who had bought the rights. I said, "This is Mercy. You're talking to her." So Courtney and I ended up meeting in front of a pizza place, and we talked for hours. I thought she was kind of dingy and very full of herself, even back then, but she pretended I was normal and I appreciated that. I think she was probably very drugged up, although we didn't do drugs together. She was just very friendly to me. And to be honest, I thought she was a lot like me. She probably would have been fantastic in the Mercy role. The last time I saw Courtney, she still wasn't known yet. It was on the bus. She was a stripper on her way to work, and she was talking about this guy Kurt Cobain. She gave me her phone number, but I lost it.

But this stuff keeps happening, now. My reputation still follows me around. Just a couple years ago Dave Davies for some reason wanted me at his gig at the Roxy. He demanded that our mutual friend invite me. It was crazy. I was saying, "What am I doing here? I barely even know this guy!" And he told me, "I just *had* to have Miss Mercy here." I have a photo from that night.

At a fortieth anniversary event for X at the Grammy Museum, Exene Cervenka gave me and Pamela a shoutout from the stage, saying, "It's really cool to have you both here tonight, because you are people that are...well, I was going to say 'pioneers,' but I think it's different from that. It's just people who had the nerve to do something that no one else was doing." When Quentin Tarantino's *Once Upon a Time...in Hollywood* came out, *Los Angeles Magazine* dedicated a full page to the GTOs in its 1969 nostalgia issue. And in Portland there's this Alice Cooper-inspired musical, *Shock Opera*, in which my doppelgänger comes to life on the stage of the Paris Theater. I found out about it when one day this girl dressed *just* like me circa '69 scrolled across my Facebook feed. For an instant, I actually thought it was an old photograph of myself that I couldn't remember. This actress, Bethany Ziskind, recreated my persona perfectly, right down to my layered glad-rags and eyeliner-smeared scowl.

The fact that anyone still is inspired by my fashion is thrilling. Recently I was invited to star in an American Apparel Halloween commercial with Alaska Thunderfuck, the marvelous winner of *RuPaul's Drag Race All Stars 2*—I wore a slinky leopard catsuit, blonde wig, and cat ears, and honestly, other than the ears, it was an outfit I'd wear any day of the week. Shortly after that, Pamela and I were invited by Alexa Chung to the famous Paramour Estate for the launch of Alexa's GTOs-inspired "Muse" clothing line. It was a surreal, floating dream to walk into this grand mansion and see the stunning Alexa and all her twenty-something "it" girl friends, like the HAIM sisters and Arrow de Wilde from the rising garage-punk band Starcrawler, paying homage to us. The party even had a photo booth area set up to look like the set of the GTOs' famous black-and-white *Rolling Stone* session Baron Wolman did in 1968, with the fancy scenester guests decking themselves out in Alexa's flowing, printed maxi dresses and ostrich boas and flower crowns, and renowned modern-day photographer Brantley Gutierrez working the camera. Later, Arrow and her boyfriend, the photographer and director Gilbert Trejo (son of Danny), invited me over to their place for dinner and paid me to pose for an artsy fisheye-lens photo in front of their red-lit bathroom's mirror; the resulting image became the artwork for Starcrawler's single "She Gets Around."

Back when I was those girls' age, I worked really hard to dress to kill and get my look just perfect. So to have that recognition now feels like winning a Grammy. It's not about a paycheck. It was never about that for me. It was just about the respect. If I could have any award that I could put on my mantel, it would be my Brantley Gutierrez photograph with Alexa Chung from that night.

I've lived most of my life believing that I was protected, but perhaps I'm finally getting my big payback for that now as I deal with all the things I've done that have resulted in permanent damage to my body and brain. Hardly anything scares me, but I'd be lying if I didn't admit I'm frightened now. By the time this book comes out, I'll still be dealing with all my damage. Or I'll be dead. But then again, it was reported that I died years ago; all the rock magazines used to print that salacious rumor every time I got arrested or OD'd. That made me feel like a ghost already—a ghost chained to the past, present, and future, just like that song I wrote. Still, it is the future that keeps me going. I don't have any life-flashing-before-my-eyes epiphanies or regrets. I don't have a bucket list. I've done everything. I would like to meet Bob Dylan again. My biggest wish in life is I would like to make amends with Shuggie and especially Lucky. And that's about it.

And so, when people ask me what the happiest time of my crazy life was, my answer is always this: I hope it hasn't even happened yet.

THE END

AFTERWORD

by Pamela Des Barres

WHEN YOU LOSE A best friend, one you've had for more than fifty years, so much of your very self is lost that it's impossible to calculate or articulate the empty place within, but I'm going to make the attempt. My beloved Miss Mercy passed in July 2020, and at least once an hour I recall a gem of hers like a ragged sparkling prism through the haze of Now. I called her blurts "Mercyisms," and there are too many to relay—she made a mess of language and created her own words. One of my favorites: She called Quentin Tarantino "Quentintino!"

It's just unimaginable that she's no longer going to sit hunched up on my couch in one of her many leopard jackets, complaining of the cold even though it's eighty degrees outside, dredging up some wacky conspiracy theory about how Otis Redding or Jimi Hendrix had been murdered by their record companies or how the government was being run by Lizard People. I had long given up trying to debate her about such ideas, and just enjoyed the rabbit hole she'd drag me into. She'd often play Devil's Advocate just to be ornery.

Our history together was so vast, beginning the day we met, even though she recalls our meeting differently. It's something we'd argued about for decades. As you have read in these pages, she thinks we met at a mad-as-a-hatter artist's digs, while I recall the first moment she sashayed into Frank Zappa's Log Cabin with crystalline clarity. Frank pointed at this zaftig, multilayered, bejeweled, heavily made-up, ragtag chick, insisting, "There's your new GTO!" The Laurel Canyon Ballet Company, consisting of a pack of wild, dancing teenage girls, had just become Mr. Zappa's latest musical group, Girls Together Outrageously, and he stated that Mercy represented a much needed "bizarre element." How right he was.

By that time, Mercy had taken copious acid trips in San Francisco and was ready to take on the entire city of Hollywood. And after my initial horror at her fearsome, brazen visage, I detected her hidden sweetness, and we settled into a deep understanding, despite our seeming differences—the perky, bright-eyed, mini-dressed blonde, tightly holding hands with the kohl-eyed, menacing Gypsy maven. We were quite a team.

Some of our finest moments were spent with our mutual heroes, including the night we spent with the Stones at their Laurel Canyon rental pad. Mick, Mercy, and I were sitting on a ledge in front of the fireplace, and he leaned into her and asked if she thought I might be interested in him. She laughed and said, "Why don't you ask her? She's right here." Gram Parsons was there that night as I danced with Mick to the Stones' newest album, *Beggars Banquet*, and Mercy read Keith's tarot cards.

She was the only GTO who'd attend Gram's Flying Burrito Brothers gigs with me. One fateful stoned evening, we entered untraveled territory into the world of country music when Gram sat us down and played records by George Jones, Merle Haggard, and Waylon Jennings, enhancing our musical palate beyond measure.

Mercy Fontenot *and* Lyndsey Parker

We were the only honored guests in the studio when the Burritos recorded "Wild Horses," and we sang in the chorus of "Hippie Boy." You can hear Mercy's distinctive, slightly out-of-tune wail above all others.

I vividly recall the night she leapt out of a huge, gooey cake at Alice Cooper's "coming out" party, when she hurled the icing at all and sundry, splatting hunks of goop on the likes of Rod McKuen and Richard Chamberlain, who thought they were attending the coming out of an actual Beverly Hills debutante. As I remember it, Mercy had smoked angel dust before her big moment, believing the late Brian Jones had entered our dressing room. She screeched, "Brian Jones, I demand that you appear before me!" In her dazzled mind, when a hapless blond kid walked in, he became the Rolling Stones' founder and she crawled over to him, wrapping her arms around his legs, refusing to let the startled fellow go.

Mercy and I are inextricably linked; there is so much herstory between us. She played her very self in the cosmic, way-out film *Rainbow Bridge*, and later introduced me to the director, Chuck Wein, a brilliant hippie guru who altered my brain cells forever. And one fine day, she took me next door to meet Chuck's fine, mind-blowing neighbor Don Johnson, who turned out to be one of my great loves.

Through the many decades, no matter what wrenching madness she'd find herself in, I managed to stick by Mercy, often coming to her rescue in various ways. I spent time with her and her deeply unconventional dad, babysat her adored son Lucky for many hours, and searched high and low for her in dangerous places. There were several horrific rapes, unbelievable amounts of drugs, hitchhiking trips to the soul-brother South, her stark-raving stripper days, the punk hair-stylist madness, and years of homelessness and living out of trashcans. I often moved her in with me, saving her ass—even after she once stole my jewelry to buy drugs—and surprisingly, she managed to save mine, especially after I moved my darling mother into my house in '97. She got sober just in time to become my mother's part-time caretaker.

Mercy had a couple months of drug-freedom, and a job at Goodwill—which she proudly kept until she left this plane—so I thought it might be good for her to spend a few hours each week with my mom while I ran errands or did a little traveling. Even though she continued to be 100 percent Mercy, she'd developed a surprising streak of practicality and I trusted her implicitly. What a blessing for all it turned out to be! Mercy and my mom became quirky sidekicks, watching the soaps on TV, bickering and smoking while Mercy pushed her wheelchair around the neighborhood. They truly came to love each other, and the responsibility gave Mercy a self-respect that helped her stay clean.

Mama was a lifelong smoker who couldn't manage to quit, and as she drew her last choking breath, and reached for the heavens, Mercy was right there with me. Still holding my hand. She always signed her cards to me "From here to eternity," and drew a crescent moon beside her signature. I could count on it. She will always be with me like a phantom limb.

It may sound zany to some, but I believe I've lived many lives with Mercy Fontenot. A psychic once told me I'd been her neglected daughter in one previous life that took place in the 1930s: She was a struggling actress, and when she was off on her auditions, she'd leave me in my crib, alone all day. I still experience occasional past-life flashbacks of the way the sun came through our venetian blinds, and how I'd know when to expect her to come back to me by the angle of the rays through the slats. It's a long story, but I wound up taking care of Mercy after her Hollywood dreams dramatically failed.

In this lifetime, she cleaned up that karma by taking good care of my mother. What a trip.

I don't know how she managed it, but Lyndsey Parker somehow captured Mercy Fontenot in these never-a-dull-moment pages, and what a wild ride of a book it is, even if some readers might be peeking through their fingers at times. It's often been difficult to keep Mercy on track, but it was extremely important to her that she be remembered, so she gave herself to Lyndsey, no holding back. In this book, her antics have been corralled and preserved—and for this I am truly grateful.

No one will ever look at me like Mercy did, and see the person only she could see. She called me her BFF, and that we shall remain. From here to eternity.

ACKNOWLEDGMENTS

Before her death on July 27, 2020, Mercy Fontenot began compiling a list of the many people she wanted to thank. That list included her son, Lucky Otis; her best friend, Pamela Des Barres; her closest friend, Cinnamon Muhlbauer; her oldest friend, Jill Lewis; her nieces, Kniqui Peters-Carbone Hackborn and Darrilyn Tharp; her ex-husband, Shuggie Otis; her GTOs sisters; and her coauthor, Lyndsey Parker.

Lyndsey Parker additionally expresses gratitude to everyone who helped make this book a reality, including Morgan and Leslie Parker, Bruce Duff, Michael Des Barres, Lol Tolhurst, Dave DiMartino, Yoshiki, Janiss Garza, Mitch Schneider, Marcee Rondan, Michael Ackerman, Arrow de Wilde, Shirley Manson, Kym Britton, Ahmet Zappa, Holland Greco, Andee Nathanson, Leslie Lewis, Libby Coffey, Ken Phillips, Lina Lecaro, Lori Majewski, Lynne Sheridan, Jasmine Lywen-Dill, Lisa Wunder, Wendy Geller, Wendy Fonarow, Meena Ysanne, Lesley Zimmerman, Jeffery Austin, Liz Garo, Frank Meyer, Mara Kuge, Katherine Turman, Toby Mamis, Eric Himmelsbach-Weinstein, Davey Havok, Alex Sax, Roger Coletti, Marcus Errico,

April McBride, Gail Champion, Tammy Kizer, Daniel House, and, of course, Tyson Cornell, Hailie Johnson, Julia Callahan, and all the wonderful people at Rare Bird. And extra special thanks to Cinnamon and Pamela...*for everything.*

ABOUT THE AUTHORS

MERCY FONTENOT, A.K.A MISS MERCY, was a member of the Frank Zappa–produced all-female band the GTOs and a fixture in the San Francisco rock revolution of the 1960s, the Memphis soul scene of the early 1970s, and the first-wave LA punk movement. She is survived by third-generation musician Lucky Otis, her son with legendary psychedelic soul artist Shuggie Otis.

Lyndsey Parker is the music editor at Yahoo Entertainment, the host of the SiriusXM's *Volume West* and Rhino Records' podcast *Totally '80s*, a regular commentator on AXS TV's *The Top Ten Revealed*, and the author of *Careless Memories of Strange Behavior: My Notorious Life as a Duran Duran Fan.*